SAVING THE TREMORS OF PAST LIVES:
A CROSS-GENERATIONAL HOLOCAUST MEMOIR

JEWS OF POLAND

Series Editor:
   Antony POLONSKY—*Brandeis University*

SAVING THE TREMORS OF PAST LIVES:
A CROSS-GENERATIONAL HOLOCAUST MEMOIR

Regina Grol

BOSTON / 2014

Library of Congress Cataloging-in-Publication Data:
A bibliographic record for this title is available from the Library of Congress.

Copyright © 2014 Academic Studies Press
All rights reserved

ISBN 978-1-61811-256-9 (cloth)
ISBN 978-1-61811-224-8 (paperback)
ISBN 978-1-61811-257-6 (electronic)

Book design by Ivan Grave. Cover design based on the artwork of Nessa Grol-Norris.

Published by Academic Studies Press in 2014
28 Montfern Avenue
Brighton, MA 02135, USA
press@academicstudiespress.com
www.academicstudiespress.com

For my mother, who meant the world to me.

*For my father, who never lost faith
in the possibility of making the world a better place.*

For my children Hanna and Ben.

And for my grandchildren, so they know.

Contents

Acknowledgments	8
Preface, by Antony Polonsky	10
Introduction	14
Chapter One: The Knight on the White Horse	16
Chapter Two: Bialystok	38
Chapter Three: From Bialystok to Dubno	59
Chapter Four: Further Migrations: From Dubno to Katowice to Haifa	66
Chapter Five: (Temporary) Return to Warsaw	77
Chapter Six: 1968; or, America! America!	86
Chapter Seven: Dreams	100
Chapter Eight: Dwelling in a Name	108
Chapter Nine: My Father: The Mystery Man	116
Chapter Ten: Mother and Her Family	127
Chapter Eleven: Danuta	144
Chapter Twelve: On Graves, Burial Rites, and the Search for Identity	148
Chapter Thirteen: Poems	162
Conclusion	168
Index	179

Acknowledgments

I am most grateful to Professors Carrie Bramen, Ann Colley, and Carolyn Korsmeyer, my friends in Buffalo, New York, who read the early drafts of the initial three chapters of this book and encouraged me to continue the project. Their positive responses were invaluable in strengthening my resolve to engage in personal writing. Professor Wilma Iggers, who read Chapter 1, also assured me of the validity of the project, as did Rachel Ariel, the Judaica librarian at Duke University, who read some of my later chapters. Profuse thanks go to all of them.

I acknowledge with gratitude the editors of *Polin: Studies in Polish Jewry* for permitting me to include my essay "1968; or America! America!," which was previously published in the 2012 issue of the journal.

The YIVO Institute for Jewish Research and the Forward Association, Inc., are hereby acknowledged for granting me permission to include my maternal great-grandfather's Mojsze Pinczuk's photograph, taken by Alter Kacyzne.

Eva Hoffman has my gratitude not only for her published works but for sharing with me her unpublished play, "The Ceremony," on the Jedwabne affair. I also wish to acknowledge Ilona Gruda of the Heritage Foundation in Montreal for letting me read her unpublished novel *Rachela*, about pre-war Warsaw, and Marta Fuchs for allowing me to quote from her published book *Legacy of Rescue: A Daughter's Tribute*.

Acknowledgments

I thank my friends, the children of survivors, who shared with me their unpublished texts as well as some of their documents and permitted me to quote them, particularly Anna Cwirko-Godycki, Anna Frajlich, and Irena Janicka-Powell. Their texts allowed me a deeper access to the experiences of the Holocaust and increased my awareness of its lingering impact.

The title of my book, *Saving the Tremors of Past Lives*, was inspired by the line "tremors of old lives" in Carolyn Kizer's translation of Rachel Korn's poem "Generations" (*Doyres*).

Profuse thanks go to Pavel Ilyin, geography consultant at the United States Holocaust Museum, who designed the map reflecting my family's peregrinations.

Crystal Reinhardt's technical assistance in producing the electronic version of my manuscript was invaluable. She has my abiding gratitude.

As a fellow at the Center for Slavic Eurasian and East European Studies at the University of North Carolina in Chapel Hill, I finally had the time and leisure to finish this book. I am extremely grateful for this opportunity.

Preface

I feel a sense of moral obligation to write about my parents' experiences. I consider it my "sacred mission," since I don't want my parents—and by extension any of the Holocaust victims—to fall out of history. I identify myself both as a conveyor of the voice of the real witnesses (i.e., my parents) and a mix of an intellectual and personal affective link with the past. I would consider silence a dereliction of my duty.

Regina Grol

This carefully crafted and deeply moving memoir is an account of the history of one of the very few Polish-Jewish families formed by the catastrophe of the Second World War and its subsequent history. Indeed, it encapsulates the history of those who survived the war and attempted to make new lives in new socialist Poland, and provides a valuable introduction to those who want to understand why it was so difficult to establish a viable Jewish community in that country after the war. Regina Grol, fellow at the Center for Slavic, Eurasian and East European Studies at the University of North Carolina, Chapel Hill, describes first how her somewhat mismatched parents survived the hell of Nazi-occupied Poland, the only members of their families to do so. Her mother, Masza Pinczuk, of a prosperous and religious family from Brześć, was able to pass as a Pole with the assistance of a sympathetic German, and worked in eastern Poland as a domestic during the years of the mass murder of the Jews. There she met her husband, Tovye (Teofil) Grol (probably an assumed name), who came from a less prosperous family, partly from Warsaw and partly from Brześć, but who had succeeded in attending a private high school, the Finkel Gymnasium, in Warsaw and in being admitted to Warsaw University before the war. A leftist, he was imprisoned before 1939 in Bereza Kartuska, and after the Nazi invasion of the Soviet Union became active in the communist partisan movement. He fell deeply in love with Masza, whom he persuaded to marry him: Regina (first Rivka), their elder child, was born four months before the end of the war. A second daughter, Halina, was born four years later. Both Masza and Teofil were Yiddish-speakers, although they also had a Polish education. Masza had a much stronger connection to her Jewish roots than did Teofil, who was above all a devoted communist. After their emigration to Paris in 1969, he wrote a novel in Yiddish, which was published in French under the title *C'est arrivé en Pologne* (Paris: Droit et Liberté, 1984), making use of his partisan experiences and describing the meeting in Italy, thirty years after the war, of the narrator and a fellow Jewish partisan from Poland.

After the war, the couple initially thought of remaining in Soviet Ukraine, but they moved back to Poland in 1946, settling first in Katowice and then in Warsaw. In both cities they were involved with Jewish organizations, such as the Towarzystwo Społeczno-Kulturalne Żydów w Polsce (the Social and Cultural Association of Jews in Poland), set up in 1950 after the communist consolidation of power in Poland to co-ordinate Jewish life and organize a Jewish culture on a socialist basis. The family emigrated to Israel in 1957, but Teofil, with his survivor background, Yiddish cultural links, and leftist politics found the country uncongenial and persuaded his wife to move back to Poland in 1959. Subsequently they were caught up in the "anti-Zionist" campaign of 1968—Teofil was accused of talking too much about the Warsaw ghetto uprising, and Masza, a teacher of Russian, was attacked by her students, who said that they no longer wanted to learn a "Jewish language." Indeed, the family was very conscious throughout its life in post-war Poland of the persistence of antisemitism. Regina's parents resettled in France in 1969, where her father was briefly affiliated with the Centre National de Recherche Scientifique in Paris and then became a freelance journalist writing in both French and Yiddish. Regina herself moved to the United States, where she became established as an expert on Polish and Polish-Jewish literature, while her sister Halina, who married an Italian, established herself in Perugia.

She concludes her memoir with a series of painful reflections on her own situation and on her identity as a Jew and a Pole. In the poem "Anchored in Ether?," she reflects on the fact that she can find HOME on her computer screen but that:

> I've clicked on it
> in ten cities
> in the past few months.
> I have clicked on it
> wherever I was.
> There are many nomads like me.
> We experience change
> all the time.
> We sense change
> both internal and external ...
> How can we anchor ourselves?
> Is the 'HOME' our only home now?

She is pained, too, by the persistence of suffering and injustice after the Holocaust.

> How conveniently we forget.
> How good we've become
> at ignoring the pain.
> How eagerly we travel
> oblivious to the pervasive
> —buried and not buried—
> presence of pain.

Yet, the memoir ends on a hopeful note. First it evokes Regina's father and mother. To her father she writes:

> I'm walking the streets of Warsaw.
> You are no longer among us…
> I sense being woven in mysterious ways
> into the fabric of history.
> Why am I here?
> What am I to do here?
> I listen and look for signs.
> I hope my words reach you …

She recalls her mother's goodness:

> Philosophers persistently
> wrestle with the question—
> *unde malum?*
> Where does evil come from?
> I am obsessed by the reverse.
> Where does goodness come from?
>
> How could my Mother,
> given her travails,
> remain so generous of spirit,
> so loving and magnanimous?
> How did she,
> a veteran of many forays
> behind the barbed wires
> of the ghetto fence,
> she whose world was shuttered,
> who was shot at,
> who cheated death by a hair,
> she who was denied bread
> when starving
> and pregnant with me,
> how did she retain
> her respect for humanity,
> her indissoluble capacity to love,
> her drive to carry on ?
> *Unde bonum?*

These two poignant reflections are followed by a conclusion and an epilogue, "LIFE GOES ON…", which consists of two photographs, one of the author's daughter, her husband, and their three children, the other of her son and his wife on their wedding day. Life does indeed go on.

Antony Polonsky

Introduction

> "The past is never dead. It's not even past."
> —William Faulkner, *Requiem for a Nun*

The impact of the Holocaust on the subsequent generation is generally recognized by now. As a child of Holocaust survivors, I was inevitably forced to examine my "pre-history." My past continuously informed my present and shaped my inner sense of identity. Attempts to escape the past were totally futile. I have long felt an overwhelming compulsion to relate to my parents' wartime experiences, which had a powerful effect not only on them, but—differently, to be sure—on me as well. I totally agree with the statement that "who you are today is a ghost of your past...."[1]

My goal in writing this book was primarily to honor my parents' memory, and to prevent their experiences from disappearing in the mists of time. Yet I have also undertaken the task as a *flaneur*, to use Walter Benjamin's term. I decided to take a retrospective look at my life, a contemplative mental stroll, in an attempt to probe my own journey through life as a child of survivors. Thus, the book is a reflection of my "internal *flanerie*," with my narrative touching on my parents' background and vicissitudes, as well as an examination of my own life against the background of post-World War II Europe, my short stays in Israel, and my decades of living in the United States.

I have resorted to essays which are windows into my parents' past and mine. While the narrative arc of this volume is not straightforward, particularly in the second half, where the recounting is not rendered chrono-

---

[1] Prabal Gurung, "Embracing the Ghosts of a Faraway Past," *The New York Times* (Sunday Styles section, February 2, 2012): 1.

logically, ultimately the narrative coalesces, I believe, into a coherent whole. In most chapters I have recorded the family's history in a personal and intimate way, but in some I could not escape donning the hat of a scholar. I have also included a few poems of mine which convey the quintessence of my legacy.

The reminiscences and assorted references included in my chapters have been vetted to the best of my ability. I have made use of documents, letters, and photographs at my disposal, extensive research, and interviews, including videotaped interviews with my mother conducted jointly by my daughter and me.

Having moved more than twenty times, and with my family dispersed on four continents, I treat my writing as an attempt to nest psychologically and to find existential moorings, a kind of "home" within. Yet my book is not a therapeutic memoir: it goes beyond that. I hope that it is, at least in a small way, a contribution to knowledge about the Holocaust and its lingering impact on the children and grandchildren of survivors.

Chapter One

The Knight on the White Horse

I have known from an early age that both of my parents were Holocaust survivors. I knew it from overheard conversations with their friends, from my parents' direct accounts, which included references to the many lost relatives, and from the many books on the Holocaust lying around our apartment. I remember looking at albums even before I could read, seeing photographs of crematoria, piled-up human corpses, and emaciated, skeleton-like human beings liberated from concentration camps. As an adult I read more on the subject, referred to it in my teaching, and certainly engaged in the Holocaust intellectually. Yet it wasn't until my forties that I experienced an overwhelming sense of wonder at the miracle of my birth, at my existence against all odds.

Although I had known that the implementation of Hitler's "Final Solution," the mass murder of all Jews, began almost immediately after the Wannsee conference of January 1942, three years before I was born, that gas chambers operated until very shortly before my birth, that Auschwitz was evacuated just one day before I was born in January 1945, and that death marches continued for several month after I was born, until April 1945, my strong emotional reaction to these facts came rather late in my life. So did my full realization of the enormity of the crimes committed by the Nazis and the magnitude of what had to be forgiven. To borrow a line from Lucille Clifton's poem, "The past was waiting for me."[1]

---

[1] Lucille Clifton, quoted from the poem "i am accused of tending to the past." http://www.poemhunter.com/i-am-accused-of-tending-to-the-past/.

Contemplating my presence in the world, I thought of my mother, swept up in the horror of the Holocaust, of her survival, and of the man who saved her life and by saving it enabled mine. If it weren't for him, I would not be here to write these words. Likewise, my sister would not have been born, nor would our children and grandchildren. The world would be deprived of our bright children's contributions.

"Whoever saves a single life is as if he has saved the entire world," says the Talmud. To paraphrase, he who saved my mother's life saved our world. His intervention was a momentous event in my mother's life and ours.

I actually met him as a child, without realizing then the significance of the encounter. I remember distinctly my family's arrival in Vienna in the spring of 1957, en route from Poland to Israel. I was twelve years old, and this was my first exposure to the West. Rather than possessing visual images of the elegant city, with its impressive buildings and beautiful parks, I have retained certain sensory impressions: the smell of a small grocery store, for instance, where I was sent, having first been coached in how to say the necessary few phrases in German. I can remember to this day how I savored the aromas of ground coffee and ripening bananas, exotic fruits I had never seen before.

I also recall the café where we met a tall man whom my mother introduced to me and my sister with these words, "This gentleman saved my life during the war." Until then, we had never heard of this man. Most likely my mother did not want us to know that she was saved by a German—it would have been politically incorrect in post-World War II Poland, where Germans were demonized in newsreels, movies, and publications. There was little tolerance then for a more nuanced view of history.

Not knowing German at the time, I could not follow my parents' conversation with the tall man. Yet I do recall the civility of the occasion and the exchange of gifts at the Vienna café. My parents came bearing a radio and a crystal vase. He, in turn, gave them a little figurine of a white horse and a book.

Now, decades later, with the painful task of liquidating my parents' apartment behind me, I am in possession of the gifts from the gentleman we met in Vienna.

I hold the book he gave my parents in my hands. The title, *Die Lüneburger heide* (The Lüneburger Heath), in white gothic font, is at the very bottom of the hard cover. Above it is a black and white photograph of a stony field, with a few poplars swaying in the wind. The picture has yellowed with age. I leaf quickly through the book, examining the snapshots of the German countryside and marveling at the unique architecture of the farm houses and barns. As I leaf back, my eyes rest on the dedication:

"Der lieben Familie Grol zur freundlichen Erinnerung an unser Wiedersehen und das Ein ander naher kennen lernen in der schoenen Stadt Wien

Herzlichst
Hermann Meyer
Wien, d.19. April 1957."

(To the dear Grol family as a friendly souvenir of our meeting and getting to know each other in the beautiful city of Vienna.

Most cordially,
Hermann Meyer
Vienna, April 19, 1957.)

Chapter One | The Knight on the White Horse

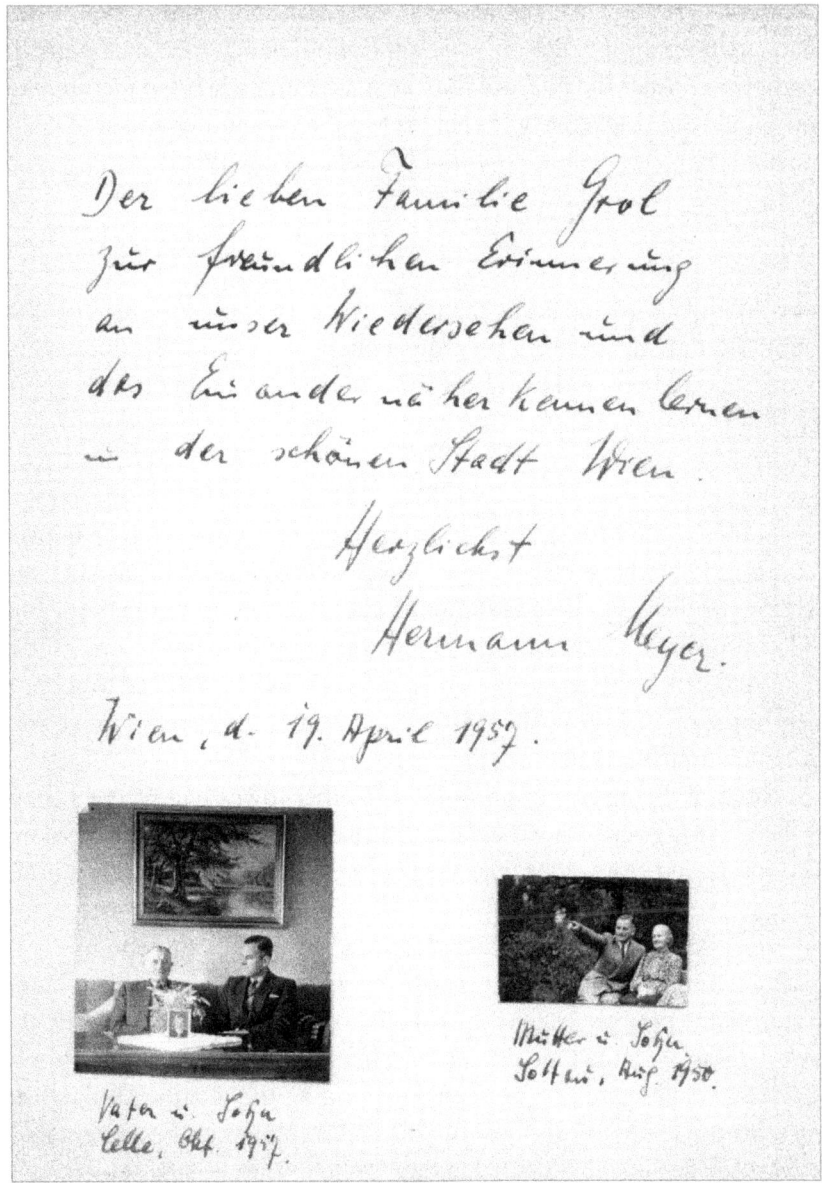

The dedication takes up the upper two thirds of the page. Two little photographs are pasted on to the lower third of the page. On the left is a small square one, showing an older and a younger man sitting next to each other on a sofa under a framed landscape painting; on the right is an even smaller rectangular photograph of the same young man and an older woman sitting on a bench in what appears to be a garden or a park. The inscriptions under the pictures indicate where and when the pictures were taken and read respectively "father and son" and "mother and son." (*Vater u. Sohn, Celle, Feb.1957; Mutter u. sohn, Soltan. Aug. 1950*).

* * *

Why did my family meet this man in Vienna? How did the meeting come about? Here are my answers, pieced together from my recollections, stories my mother told me, and her notes and letters which I found.

* * *

My mother's native town, Brześć, which today is the border town between Poland and Belarus, is called Brest Litovsk in Russian and Belarussian, and Brisk in Yiddish. The liquidation of its ghetto began on October 15, 1942, and continued for several days. Some weeks earlier, my future mother, Masza Pinczuk, age twenty-one, and her family had been forced to abandon their house on 31 Listowskiego Street, and were made to move into a small apartment in the ghetto.

News of the mass murder of Jews in other towns had reached Brześć by then, so my grandfather, Lejb Pinczuk, and my mother's brother Szlomo, who was eleven years older than she was, secretly began preparing a hiding place.

They started digging under the floor in one of the rooms in the apartment and were hoping to reach a garden shed, where they planned to store some provisions. Stealthily removing the dug-up soil at night, they kept digging intently. One day, sooner than expected, a growing number of German soldiers could be seen surrounding the ghetto. Although the work on the "bunker" was hardly finished, my mother, her parents, and her brother decided to hide in that dug-up hole. The Gestapo showed up so unexpectedly that everybody who was in the back yard rushed inside and then descended into the hole without even bringing any water. Intended for six people (my mother's family and a widowed neighbor with her child), the bunker ended up "housing" seventeen: my grandparents were too kindhearted to refuse entry to some other hounded Jews.

A day earlier, on October 14, Mrs. Grzegżołko, a shopkeeper whose son was employed as a policeman, approached the ghetto fence looking for Masza, whom she knew quite well—on various forays outside the ghetto, after sneaking between barbed wires, Masza had gone to the shopkeeper and traded the family's possessions for food.

Not finding her, Mrs. Grzegżołko asked some people to let Masza know that tomorrow *będzie źle* (there'll be trouble), and that she should bring as many valuable items as possible to Mrs. Grzegżołko's store while she still could. My mother got the message, but ignored it. There had been many warnings before, all of which turned out to be false alarms. Indeed, almost daily some Poles would shout across the ghetto fence—*jutro was wyrżną* (tomorrow they'll slaughter you). Unfortunately, this time the warning was right, and the slaughter did begin on October 15, 1942.

* * *

Packed so tightly in the dug-out hole that they could barely move, the people hiding there abandoned shame. My maternal grandmother Rifka had to sit on the loaf of bread she had brought along, for there was no other place to put it. Unfortunately, with the shooting and screaming all around, and being herself unable to move and afraid to leave, she—like all the others—had to relieve herself where she sat. The emergency supplies became useless.

The first night, my grandfather, Lejb Pinczuk, snuck out and brought back a jar of water. Each person was allowed only one sip. A young mother conceded her sip to her three-year-old daughter, the girl had moaned all night and had kept asking if the mother had any breast milk left.

The situation in the bunker deteriorated rapidly. The starved, oxygen-deprived, and dehydrated people began literally losing their minds. Another mother, who had brought her baby to the bunker and could not stop his crying, was forced by the people sitting next to her to cover the baby's mouth when a German patrol was heard nearby. This prevented the Germans from discovering the bunker, and the lives of the remaining people were saved (only for a while, as it turned out), but the baby suffocated. The mother was despondent and raving.

Another woman began shrieking and cursing her long-deceased husband, accusing him of infidelities. Masza's brother Szlomo became delirious and started pulling her hair, mistaking her for a cat. Masza herself had a delusional vision of a bird sitting on her brother's leg.

At night, overcoming her fear, Masza ventured out to bring back some food and water. She approached the fence and managed to sneak out under the barbed wire, but a Pole grabbed her and took away her watch and the necklace she was going to exchange for food. She return to the bunker, took some other possessions, and rushed to Mrs. Grzegżołko's house. [2]

The shopkeeper took one look at the skinny and frightened girl and asked her to stay, to live with her and help around the store. A strong sense of loyalty to her family kept my mother from accepting the offer. She declined, asked Mrs. Grzegżołko for food, then hurried back to the ghetto to deliver the bread and milk she had been given. Alas, totally dehydrated in the overcrowded and stuffy hole, the people in the bunker could not even drink the milk. It would not quench their thirst; they kept asking for water. Masza ventured out again. Little did she know that this would be the last time she would see this temporary home.

On this excursion a Pole wearing a German uniform caught her and put a gun to her head. She started pleading with him for her life: told him that she was too young to die; that she knew his friends from school; that as a Christian he should be merciful. He ignored her pleas and finally hissed, *"Jak ja cię puszczę to mnie kula w łeb"* (If I let you go, I'll get a bullet in the head). Sensing his intransigence, Masza started running as fast as she could. He fired at least three bullets in her direction. She told me numerous times of the bullets missing her by less than an inch, of the heat she felt on her skin as they flew by, of her tongue stiffening, of the tightening of her throat. (Was the policeman inept, I wonder today, or did he miss her deliberately?)

Her nerves completely wrecked, Masza kept running toward the shopkeeper's house. At one point, as she touched her head, she realized that her hair was standing on end and as much as she tried, she could not make it fall in place. Terrified that her unusual appearance would betray her, Masza darted into a dark passage and, as she had nothing else with

---

[2] As I read Henryka Lazowert's poem engraved on a wall at the entrance to the Jewish Cemetery in Warsaw, a poem in praise of the child smuggler, I could envision my mother in that role. I bowed my head, honoring her and the children in many ghettoes who risked their lives to save their families from starvation.

which to cover her head, she pulled off her underwear and created a kind of turban. It fell off as she continued to run, but she succeeded in reaching Mrs. Grzegżołko's home. She knew that it was now too dangerous for her to return to her family.

The compassionate woman received Masza warmly. She fed her, gave her a bath, washed her hair, and even deloused her. Despite the repeated offer to remain and help around the store, Masza declined and asked only to stay for the night. The next day, when some German soldiers showed up in Mrs. Grzegżołko's yard, the shopkeeper began to stutter. She realized then that despite her good intentions she would be unable to keep her cool and would endanger her family by keeping a Jewish girl in the house.

As soon as the soldiers were gone, Masza herself offered to leave. Mrs. Grzegżołko remained silent, but her son suggested hiding Masza in the cellar. Utterly exhausted by her experiences in the ghetto, and with the sound of the bullets still ringing in her ears, my future mother had reached a state of emotional numbness. She had no desire to live. All she wanted was to spare her hosts any harm. The only request she made of the Grzegżołko family was to find a German who would shoot her and end her misery. All too readily, Mrs. Grzegżołko agreed to grant Masza's request.

The shopkeeper was about to go and summon a German soldier she knew when her husband intervened, declaring that he would find a better solution and forbidding his wife to leave the house. He went out and returned two hours later in the company of a Pole employed by the railroad company, who knew the train schedules by heart. "Where do you want to go?" the man asked my mother.

Where was she to go? Exhausted, penniless, never exposed to the larger world, and aware only of the imminent threat from both the Poles and the Germans, Masza chose Wysokie Litewskie, a nearby town, where she had relatives (her paternal grandmother, an uncle, two aunts, and cousins).[3] The man promised to return and take her to the railway station when it would get dark.

In the meantime, Mrs. Grzegżołko set out to bleach Masza's hair with peroxide. She also made her a ham sandwich for the road and equipped her with a cheap plastic crucifix on a chain to be worn around the neck. Most importantly, she gave Masza a student ID for the school year 1937-

---

[3] The Russian name of the town is Vysoko-Litovsk and the Belorussian name is Vysokoye.

1938 issued to a girl by the name of Maria Naliwajkówna, born in 1922. My mother, born on December 24, 1921, was roughly the same age. Thus, to quote my mother, she left the shopkeeper's house "as a freshly-baked Aryan."

The railway employee kept his word. He came back and led Masza to the station, having previously made arrangements with a conductor to let her ride a night train. He instructed her to board the last car of the next train, and showed her some bushes where she could hide until then.

Winter came early that year. While Masza was sitting behind the bushes, shivering from cold, a patrol of two German soldiers accompanied by a dog passed by. Probably attracted by the scent of the ham sandwich, the dog came within inches of her face and started barking, baring its teeth. Masza was petrified. She was convinced that this was her end. But caught up in their conversation, the soldiers ignored the barking. They summoned the dog and, well trained, it obeyed and followed them.

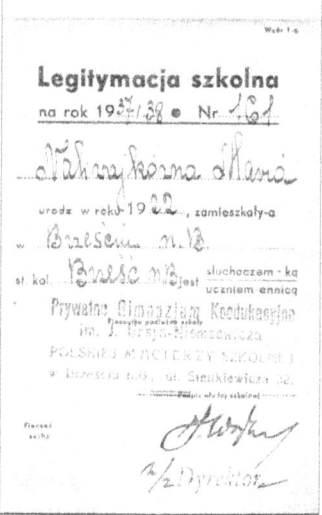

My mother's nervous reaction to this scare, as she told me on various occasions, was thirst, "wild thirst," as she put it. To quench it, she rushed out of her hiding place to look for something—anything—to drink. She found a rusty sardine can on the railway track and drank its contents, not knowing, in her words, "whether it was rain water or a dog's urine."

The train finally arrived. As instructed, Masza boarded the last car in the dark of the night. The date was October 25, 1942. When the train stopped at the next station, she saw young girls loading enormous packs of shoes and clothing onto the cargo car. My mother realized at once these had once been the belongings of the murdered Jews.

***

Worn out by her escape from the Brześć ghetto, the subsequent tensions, her surreptitious entry into the train, and the fear throughout the ride that fellow passengers might find her out, Masza made it to Wysokie Litewskie. No one else got off at that snow-covered station. As she walked on the deserted platform and approached the station master's window, she could hear him exclaim, "Where the hell did she come from?"

Although she was exhausted, famished, and barely able to walk, Masza made an effort to leave the train station as fast as she could, but in a matter of minutes she collapsed into a snow embankment on a nearby street. Despite the cold, she decided to take a nap then and there. Her respite was short-lived: moments later a young man came by and poked her. She could sense he was not a Good Samaritan; his intent was most likely to denounce her. Emboldened by her possession of Maria Naliwajkówna's ID, Masza put up a front and told him with much assurance that she came to town to buy a coat. She had been told one could buy coats very cheaply from the Jews, so she came to get one at the Wysokie Litewskie ghetto, she declared. Would he show her the way? As a gesture of good will she offered him the sandwich prepared by Mrs. Grzegżołko. (In those days, my future mother observed the dietary laws of *kashruth* very strictly. That is why, despite her hunger, she had not eaten the ham sandwich.) The young man took the sandwich and examined it. Perhaps seeing the pork inside the roll he concluded that she could not be Jewish. In any case, he pointed her in the general direction and left.

At the crack of dawn, after repeatedly getting lost in the unfamiliar streets of Wysokie Litewskie, Masza passed a group of Jews being led to forced labor outside the ghetto. She asked directions of them and finally made it to the ghetto.

Once there, she located her cousin Inda Nirenblat, who was quite eager to hear Masza's account of the Brześć relatives. However, when she found out that, except for Masza's married older sister Chaja and her little son Szalomek, the remaining members of Masza's immediate family were still alive, Inda expressed regret that her own immediate family had been either deported or killed by the Germans while Masza's was spared.[4]

---

4   Chaja and her son perished in the Kovel ghetto. I write about their death in the chapter "Dreams."

This reaction did not sit well with my mother. Inda must have sensed that, or perhaps she just did not want to share her small quarters, so she took Masza to Uncle Lejzor's place.

Lejzor, my maternal grandfather's younger brother, had a small one-bedroom apartment furnished with a medium sized bed, where he and his wife slept, and a crib for their toddler. Upon her arrival, the boy was taken to his parents' bed, and Masza slept in the crib, with her legs protruding more than a foot.

The child would repeatedly wet the bed during the night, so his parents had to get up to change the sheets. Masza felt ill at ease inconveniencing them so much. Worse yet, with her relatives preoccupied with their own survival, she felt like an intruder and had a sense of overpowering loneliness. Within a week of her arrival in Wysokie Litewskie, she decided to leave it. By then, the ghetto was already surrounded by German soldiers in preparation for its liquidation.

My mother found herself trapped again. She attempted to get out, relying on the same fabricated story which had saved her before. Again she claimed that she was Catholic and had come to the ghetto to buy a coat. Moving along the perimeters of the ghetto, she addressed one soldier after another across the barbed wire fence, appealing to them to let her out, but to no avail. Although she addressed them in German, they all ignored her. Then the unexpected happened.

A knight on a white horse, or a prince on a white horse, is the proverbial dream of many young girls. Well, my mother's dream came literally true during this, one of the most difficult moments of her life. As she was losing all hope of leaving the ghetto and surviving, a tall, handsome man in uniform, riding a white horse, stopped in front of the ghetto gate. After watching her attempts to engage the soldiers, the man asked in German, "What does the girl want?" A soldier repeated Masza's claim. Whether it was her appearance, the tone of her voice, or her determination that made the rider notice her in the crowd she never knew, but he turned out to be Hauptmann (captain) Hermann Meyer, the chief of the local military police. He gave the order to lead my mother out and bring her to the police station for interrogation. The policeman standing closest to him, *Zugwachtmeister* (railway guard) Schrider, obeyed instantly and, holding a gun to the back of Masza's head, brought her to the police station. Along the way, she pleaded with him to kill her. What was the point of dragging her to the police station, she asked. For him, however, an order was an order, and in a gruff voice he kept saying "*Nein*" (No).

They reached the police station, which had formerly been the palace of Count Potocki. Masza was left alone in a waiting room, where she sat motionless, resigned to death, for two hours. At last the chief of police returned to the station, and she was led into the interrogation room. Three men—Hauptmann Meyer, Schrider, and yet another German, "with a bandit's face," as my mother described him—were staring at her. They took her ID and began interrogating her closely. Asked about her parents' whereabouts, she replied that her entire family had been deported to Siberia by the Soviets. She was without a permanent home, she told them, and supported herself by working for people in exchange for food and lodging.

Mother around 1940.
Picture from the Yad Vashem Archive

She came to the ghetto hoping to buy an inexpensive winter coat. While she had memorized all the data on the ID and answered questions pertaining to it correctly, she did not resemble the girl in the picture at all. The shape of her nose was different, which the men noticed instantly and commented on. Even her short hair was in sharp contrast to the two long braids of the girl in the picture. When asked about the braids, Masza, being quick on her feet, responded that cutting one's hair upon high school graduation was a local custom.

The men had serious suspicions. By the end of the hour-long interrogation, Masza saw the man with the bandit's face pass a note with the word *Spione* (spy) to Hauptmann Meyer. Yet, as the commanding officer of "5-Pol-2," Meyer had the final word, and he gave the order to send my mother to work in the kitchen, pending further investigation. (I have subsequently learned, doing research at the United States Holocaust Museum, that the mysterious abbreviation in the officer's title referred to the 5th Battalion of Police Regiment II stationed in Wysokie Litewskie.)

The kitchen served about 150 military police. In one of Mother's notebooks written in Polish (she began writing her memoir, but, alas, never finished it), I found this description of her kitchen work:

> There were two vats filled with potatoes. A young Polish woman was already at work. I sat down next to her and started peeling potatoes from the other vat. An hour later, I had a big pile peeled. She had considerably fewer. The kitchen supervisor walked in, picked up a few potatoes from the Polish girl's vat and yelled at her: "Look how the other girl is peeling! Look how thin her peels are and there are no 'black eyes' on the potatoes. And the ones you've peeled are almost square. Your pile of peels is impressively high, but there are hardly any potatoes left!"
>
> (I owed my "art" of peeling potatoes thinly, not wastefully, to my father, Lejb Pinczuk, who in his youth had worked as a forest ranger and had the task of marking trees to be cut and delivered to his father's saw mill. Traversing the vast forests owned by my grandfather, Mojsze Pinczuk, he had to fend for himself, so he acquired assorted skills, which he imparted to his children.)[5]
>
> My fingers hurt from peeling the potatoes, but I was alive.
>
> That was the only thought that I was then clinging to; I could think of nothing else. Eventually, the cook gave me some black ersatz coffee and some noodles. They were covered with lard, and I almost chocked on them. Minutes later, I was ordered to wash some big military pots, dice the potatoes, and mop the kitchen floor.
>
> Late at night, a soldier led me through the snow covered streets to a Polish policeman's house. His family of four slept in the kitchen, where it was warm. The policeman's wife showed me to a room which had never been heated. I was freezing and convinced that the next day I would surely not elude death.

---

[5] My great-grandfather, Mojsze [pronounced Moysheh] Pinczuk of Wysokie Litewskie, owned extensive forests and routinely exposed his children to nature. Despite his rabbinical ordination, my grandfather Lejb Pinczuk, a lover of the outdoors, opted to work for his father as a *brakarz*, that is, one who traverses the woods and marks trees for cutting. I write more about both Mojsze Pinczuk and Lejb Pinczuk in the chapter titled "Mother and her Family."

I couldn't sleep. I stretched out on my bed, with all my clothes on, and was thinking about the speech I would make before I would die. I composed it in German in my head. It was a touching, yet accusatory speech.

I knew German fairly well: I had studied it for four years in high school, and even tutored other pupils. Elegantly-dressed women, some of them wives of army officers, would come to my mother and inquire whether I could tutor their children, who were failing the subject. In the spring of my last year of high school, I tutored four boys (Krzaczkowski, Machowski, and two others whose names I can't remember) in German, and one girl, Janka Lecykówna, in all the school subjects.

Tutoring earned me 55 zlotys a month. My parents were very proud of me, of course, and I was glad because all of my students made it to the next grade. I even got a present—10 zlotys—from Janka's parents in addition to my payment.

Considering my abilities, I thought I'd put my knowledge of German to good use.

Early in the morning, Zugwachmeister Schrider came to take me back to the police station. The first words I addressed to him were, "Are you going to kill me?" He calmed me down and took me back to the kitchen. I began to work at once. Suddenly Hauptmann Meyer walked in. He was tall and appeared to me haughty, a proud representative of the "superior race." I learned later that he routinely came to the kitchen to taste and approve the food. Hauptmann Meyer gave the order that I should be given some breakfast and announced that he and Schrider were going to Brześć to check out my background. Later, as he was leaving, he quietly said to me that he would leave no guards to watch me. Was he giving me a hint? I wondered, yet I wasn't sure. In any case, where could I escape to? I had no strength left to defy death, which seemed to follow me wherever I went. I spent the whole day frozen with fear, yet I continued to assist in the kitchen and peel potatoes.[6]

My mother retained a callus under the index finger of her right hand for the rest of her life. I remember seeing it and feeling it when she stroked me.

Around 8 p.m., "Maria" was allowed to go back to the Polish policeman's home. As soon as she entered her cold room, extremely tired

---

[6] This and all subsequent quotations from my mother's writings are in my translation from the Polish. R.G.

after the previous sleepless night and the long hours in the kitchen, not to mention her inner tension, she stretched on her bed fully dressed and fell asleep. Loud knocking woke her up less than an hour later. She got up quickly and opened the door, assuming instantly that someone had come with her death warrant and that these were the last moments of her life. Hauptmann Meyer's attendant, Mr. Kozlowsky, was at the door. An elderly and simple-minded German, he was sent to summon my mother to a late night interrogation.

As she wrote in her notebook, *"I don't know how I mustered the strength to walk, or what force brought me to Hauptmann Meyer's office. I arrived there half dead."*

The interrogation began with Meyer reporting with a smile that, while in Brześć, he had met the priest who had baptized Maria Nalewajkówna and her twin sister. The existence of a twin sibling came as a huge surprise to my mother. During the ensuing questioning, much as she tried, she could not hide her ignorance. She managed only to come up with a cockamamie story about her parents divorcing when she was very little and never telling her about the twin. She had been raised by her mother, she claimed, so perhaps her father took the other child.

Asked about the mother's first name, she replied that it was Stefania. While that was a much more Christian-sounding name than Rifka, her real mother's name, it turned out, alas, to be a wrong one. Confronted regarding this error, my mother dwelt on the distinction between birthdays and name days and ultimately came up with another improbable story that her mother used a nickname and no one ever called her by her given name. It was becoming increasingly obvious that the ID was not hers.

At that point, there was a knock on the door. Hauptman Meyer left the room. During his short absence, Masza noticed a postcard from his mother on the desk. Not daring to touch it, she read it nevertheless, and memorized the sender's address in Celle-beim-Hanover.

Upon his return a few minutes later, Meyer caught her looking at the postcard. He flipped it over, revealing a picture of Beethoven. "Do you know who this is?" he asked. Having learned about the composer at school, my mother identified him instantly and commented on his life. Whether it was her fluent German that impressed him, or the fact that she knew about a composer born near what he claimed as his native town, or perhaps because of the glowing reports about her work in the kitchen (where she had advanced to peeling onions and other vegetables requiring skillful work), it is impossible to say, but he handed her the baptismal certificate of Maria Nalewajkówna and an affidavit that her parents and grandparents had been practicing Catholics. Mr. Kozlowsky was instructed to take her back to the Polish policeman's home. My mother was now in possession of solid Aryan cover, but she still doubted that the papers would save her life.

At the end of the next day, totally drained by her work in the kitchen, "hellishly tired" (*piekielnie zmęczona*), to use her words, my mother went back to the Polish policeman's home for the night. The lights were out and the front door was locked—the family was away. After a moment of panic she located the key under the doormat and let herself in.

Minutes later, unexpectedly, a neighbor entered her room and started making advances. She kept pushing him away. He persisted, and she yelled in desperation, "Leave me alone! I'm a virgin!" Fortunately, her hosts returned in time to hear her screams and sent the neighbor away. The policeman must have reported the incident at the police station, for the next time Hauptmann Meyer and Schrider saw her they were exceedingly solicitous. She interpreted their behavior as showing their appreciation for her chastity and moral conduct.

Mother continued working in the kitchen. On one occasion, the cook asked her to deliver a carafe of water to *Zugwachtmeister* Schrider's office. As "Maria" walked in he thanked her and, in the midst of complimenting her on her work, remarked that he would never permit a Jew to serve him water, nor would he eat anything touched by a Jew; he would be too disgusted. Ironically, to quote my mother again, this is what he told her next:

> I know you have no family. It so happens, my wife and I, we don't have any children. I'll give you the address of a shoemaker in Bialystok. Wherever you are, let that shoemaker know your whereabouts. When I retire, or when the war ends, I'll come for you and adopt you as my daughter. It may be a difficult matter, but at least you would not be alone, you would be with us and could help us.

Schrider repeated this plan to my mother on several occasions. He clearly wanted her as one of his spoils of war.

Both he and Kozlowsky seemed to enjoy talking to my mother. Once, when she was sent to Meyer's quarters to mend some of his undershirts and woolen socks, Kozlowsky regaled her with rather revealing stories about his boss. Hauptmann Meyer was a mama's boy, Kozlowsky told her, a "softie," who cried in his room after some *Aktion* during which many Jews were shot. Had his boss married, he would have been promoted a long time ago, Kozlowsky declared, but being impotent, he could not find a wife. A girlfriend who had visited Meyer had gone back to Germany after two days, and from this Kozlowsky drew the firm conclusion that his boss could not satisfy her sexually.

Yet work and occasional chitchats hardly sum up my mother's life in those days. She lived in constant fear and was repeatedly traumatized. On one occasion, the cook sent her to the cellar to fetch some coals. Filling the bucket, she sensed that some pieces of coal were sticking to her fingers. When she came out of the darkness, Mother realized that her hands were covered with thick blood. While she wasn't aware at first that it was human blood, she was soon enlightened by the Polish woman who worked in the kitchen. The woman told her that a young Jew was brought in, that they had shot him several times, but he had kept running. Finally he had dashed into the cellar, and that's where they had finished him off. She gave my mother a detailed account of this incident with a smile on her face and, as my mother recalled with dismay, an expression of great satisfaction.

Another time, mother saw the ground moving—literally—at a site where a group of Jews had been buried alive. Her own report follows:

> *I was still employed in the kitchen and I was asked not to come to work the next day. I was surprised, but welcomed the opportunity to rest. About 11 a.m., terrible shooting began. I thought these were military exercises.*
>
> *The next morning, when I was on my way to work, there was white snow all around. Suddenly, I noticed a huge square area covered with black soil. It looked like the floor of a room, with single shoes, handkerchiefs, and gloves scattered around. As I approached it, I detected some movement.... I understood then why there had been so much shooting. I took a few more steps along the road, but had to sit down. I had no strength to continue on. I sat and prayed for the dead and the dying Jews. Yet very quickly I realized that now, when the liquidation of the Wysokij Litowsk ghetto was taking place, the kitchen was the safest place for me, though I knew death threatened me there as well. I cannot forget that day.*

Neither the kitchen nor the streets were safe for my mother, given her brown eyes and dark complexion. Danger lurked constantly, even around the home of the policeman where she was staying. One night she heard a gunshot followed by a guttural scream and a strange noise. She looked out the window and saw a German soldier standing over the corpse of an emaciated man who must have escaped from the ghetto. What she had heard were the dying breaths of the young Jew killed with one shot. The German soldier noticed her in the window and pointed his gun at her, but luckily, she ducked in time.

A few days later the front was moving east. Sent outside the kitchen to sweep the snow, she saw the Germans packing, loading their trucks with supplies in preparation for the following day's departure. Schrider and Meyer spoke (perhaps jokingly) of smuggling her—that is, putting her in a barrel or a wooden trunk and taking her along. This they did not do, but Hauptmann Meyer did issue her a certificate indicating that until that date she had been employed by the German military police. He did not mention in the certificate the very short duration of her employment: about ten days!

Asked by Meyer what she intended to do next, my mother replied that she would like to go to Bialystok. She did not breathe a word about he relatives—her aunt Pola Zylberblat, and her husband and daughter—who lived there, but merely said that Bialystok was a bigger city, where she would have a better chance of finding employment. Hermann Meyer instantly provided her with the address of a woman in Bialystok who rented rooms to German officers and resided on a street renamed Usidomstrasse by the Germans. He himself had stayed there and told Mother she could use him as a reference. Hauptmann Meyer's parting words to my mother were, "*Maria, Sie sind rein innerlich und auserlich*" (Maria, you are pure inside and out).

The next day Schrider delivered a ticket to Bialystok to my mother and accompanied her to the train station, where he put her in a car reserved exclusively for Germans. It was a much safer place for her than the other cars were, for arrests of Poles on trains and elsewhere, known as roundups (*łapanki*), were quite common in those days. Surrounded by German soldiers, Mother arrived in Bialystok safely. Her entire luggage consisted of her handbag, yet that handbag contained her life-saving documents.

* * *

To Mother's great surprise, a few days after her arrival Hauptmann Meyer stopped by the landlady's home on Usidomstrasse to inquire about Maria's well-being. My mother was out at the time, but was told about his visit and his expressed concern. During Meyer's next visit to Bialystok, when she had already found a job and had moved, he located her at the new address and came to reiterate Schrider's intention to adopt her after the war. On that occasion, he also paid my mother a compliment. He told her that he had sent a package of his old clothes to his mother in Germany, and having received it she had written to inquire who had mended them so nicely, being particularly impressed with the "artistically" darned socks.

It was during that visit that my mother furtively, impulsively, slipped into Hermann Meyer's pocket her last valuable possession of great sentimental value—a tiny gold watch which had been given to her by my grandmother Rifka as a high school graduation present. (That was the watch Hermann Meyer subsequently returned to my mother, and which, to continue the tradition, my mother passed on to me upon my own graduation from high school.)

* * *

To bring this part of my family's story full circle, I must move ahead several years and proceed to the post-war era. Given the atmosphere in Poland after World War II and the continued sense of danger in that country, most Jews who survived the war left Poland as soon as they could, particularly following the 1946 pogrom in Kielce. After 1949, for several years the Polish authorities closed all the borders; the iron curtain came down with a thud. It was not until the 1956 workers' riots and the subsequent change of guard in the Communist party that a political thaw began, with Jews at last being allowed to emigrate again. The typical route of Jewish émigrés involved a brief stay in Vienna for "processing" by the Hebrew Immigration Society. Next, they embarked on trains to Naples, Genoa, or another Italian port, from which most would continue to travel to Israel by boat.

My family was part of this second wave of immigration. Early in 1957, when my family decided to leave Poland, my mother wrote a letter to Hermann Meyer. She composed it in German, addressing him as *Mein*

Leben Raetter (my life-saver) and assuring him that she had never forgotten she owed her life to him. Mother informed Hermann Meyer that she was married and had two children, and that while she was in Vienna she would like to personally express her gratitude. The letter was sent to Germany, my mother having remembered for all those years the address on the postcard she had noticed during her interrogation in Wysokie Litewskie. Although Hermann Meyer had moved, the letter was forwarded to his new address.

* * *

Why did Hermann Meyer accept the invitation to Vienna? That question has often puzzled me over the years. Did he expect a reward? Did he want to ease his conscience, having undoubtedly committed many crimes during the war? Was it sheer curiosity? Was the trip to Vienna a distraction from his daily routines? The questions remain unanswered. All I do know is that he came.

I imagine that the conversation during the meeting in Vienna must have been stilted at first, but the atmosphere clearly warmed up, for he told my parents rather personal details about his life, such as that he had never married and that his mother had passed away, which caused him much pain and anguish.

If he came expecting a reward, he must have been disappointed. Having lost everything during the war, and coming as they were from an impoverished, war-ravaged country in the Eastern Block, my parents were in no position to give him much. The gifts they brought to Vienna cost them several months' salary, but from his Western perspective they must have seemed quite modest. Mother realized that she could never repay him, but she had a continuing compulsion to express her gratitude. Her subsequent attempt to do so was a resounding failure. As soon as we settled in Israel, she sent him a bottle of holy water from the Holy Land and some other religious paraphernalia blessed by the Pope. Hermann Meyer wrote to thank her, but politely informed her that he was Protestant, so he passed the gifts to his sister, who had married a Catholic.

I have also often wondered about the souvenirs Hermann Meyer gave my parents. Was the white horse a fond reminder of his days in Poland? Was it evidence of his continued passion for horses? Or had Mother mentioned in her letter to him the impression he made on her when she first saw him on his white horse? Perhaps she had mentioned her own father's love of horses? Then, too, why did Hermann Meyer paste his parents' pictures in the book he brought to Vienna? Was it because he knew he was meeting a family and wanted to show a family of his own, yet being single, with his mother dead, this was all he had to show?

Having read Bryan Mark Rigg's book *Hitler's Jewish Soldiers*, the thought has also crossed my mind that perhaps he had some Jewish blood and might have been "Aryanized" by Hitler.

I am unlikely to ever get answers to these questions, for my parents have passed away and so has Hermann Meyer. Yet to this day in my heart I am grateful to him for my mother's life and mine.

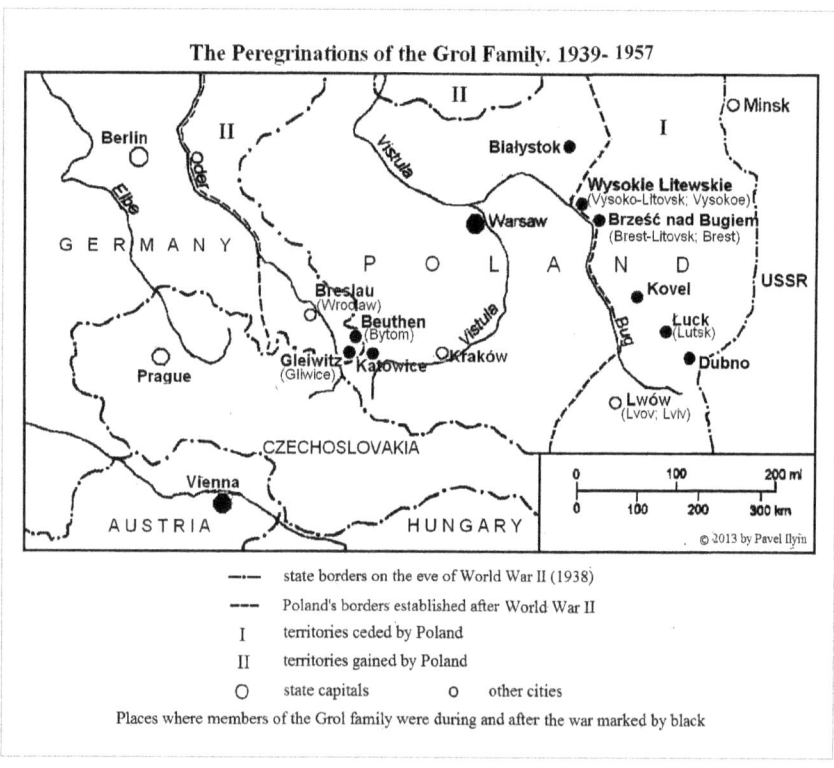

Chapter One | The Knight on the White Horse 37

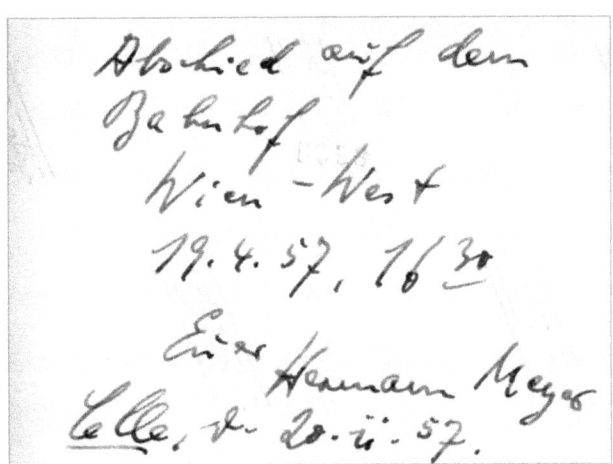

Photograph of my family taken by Hermann Meyer in Vienna. The inscription on the reverse reads:
> *Farewell at the train station Vienna West*
> *April 19, 1957, 4:30 PM*
> *Yours, Hermann Meyer*
> *Celle, Nov. 20, 1957.*

[The picture was mailed from Celle to Haifa on that date.]

Chapter Two

Bialystok

Taking a few minutes' respite from writing, I sit down to enjoy a cup of coffee and switch on my favorite radio station, NPR (National Public Radio). The first word I hear is, "Bialystok." My curiosity is piqued. The name of this Polish city is hardly ever mentioned in the US media, so I listen intently to find out the reason for Bialystok's moment in the spotlight. What I hear is the story of the "bialy," an onion-covered roll which originated in a Jewish bakery in Bialystok. According to the chef being interviewed on NPR, decades ago the baker who invented the roll immigrated to New York City, where he made the bialy popular, and its popularity has been spreading across the USA ever since. The NPR program continued, featuring other recipes and their histories, but the word Bialystok diverted my attention from culinary matters and triggered memories of a very different kind.

I have never visited Bialystok, yet it has a prominent place in my family's lore. Bialystok was the place of repeated brushes with death and profound existential fears for my parents, but it was also the city where they met, married, and were liberated.

* * *

In December 1942, upon arriving in Bialystok from Wysokie Litewskie, my mother tried to locate Miss Bisłowska at the address given to her by Hermann Meyer. She had been given instructions on how to get to the woman's house, at number 8 *Usidomstrasse* (Usidom Street, whose former Polish name had been *ulica Łukowska*), but encountered a fork in the road and was uncertain which way to go. A young Pole strolling nearby gallantly offered to show her the way when she asked him for directions. Instead of taking her to the desired address, however, he led her directly to the Gestapo. Ordered to present her identification papers, my mother promptly pulled out the documents confirmed by "5-Pol-2" (Fünf-Pol-Zwo), the military police division in Wysokie Litewsk. The Bialystok Gestapo had no basis on which to detain her. Without a word of apology, the gallant young Pole then led her to the proper address.

Miss Bisłowska turned out to be both affable and warm. A middle-aged spinster who lived with her elderly father, she had a vacant room and agreed to rent it to my mother. In fact, in no time, she treated Maria (by now my mother was used to that name) as a member of the family. The landlady was gentle, and seemed to draw on her repressed maternal instinct in dealing with her new tenant. Haunted as my mother was by her experiences in both the Brześć and the Wysokie Litewsk ghettoes, she would often toss and cry in her sleep. Miss Bisłowska would quietly come into my mother's room, stroke her, and often put an additional blanket on her if the temperature dropped. (Years later, when my mother would tell me about Miss Bisłowska, she often referred to her as "a true Christian.")

As "Maria" appeared at Miss Bisłowska's home very poorly dressed, the kind woman immediately remedied the situation. I found this passage in Mother's unfinished memoir:

> My outfit, which I wore day in and day out, consisted of a worn-out brown skirt, a gray short-sleeved sweater and a threadbare cardigan of the same color. That's what I wore in the bunker and that was all I possessed. Miss Bisłowska offered to make me a dress. She pulled out a navy blue woolen frock, which she had worn before the war as a uniform in her grocery store.
>
> She was a good seamstress and, with my help, in two hours she made me a tight navy blue skirt and a little jacket. She also made me two striped blouses out of her father's two old shirts.

These articles of clothing constituted most of my mother's wardrobe till the end of the war.

Mother participated in all the daily routines of the household, and the landlady engaged her in them most pleasantly. Yet nice as Miss Bisłowska was, Mother could not be open with her. Deeply affected by the horrors of the past weeks, she yearned to "unload," to confide in someone. But whom could she tell? Too much was at stake, and she trusted no one. All she could tell Miss Bisłowska were invented, funny stories.

Survival was challenging for my mother even while she stayed with this kind woman. There were many moments of anxiety, tension, and fear. For example, on her first Sunday in Bialystok, she was invited by Miss Bisłowska to join her at church. The mere prospect of going to a Sunday mass generated much inner stress in my mother. To quote her again,

> *I was terrified that I would give myself away somehow, or make some mistake and thus precipitate my own death. I feared someone might take a good look at me and whisper to Miss Bisłowska that I was certainly Jewish, or—worse yet—recognize me and snitch directly to the Gestapo, who would come to her home and kill us all. I went to church with my heart pounding. On the way, I came upon an idea. I took her under her arm and whispered in her ear, "I have to tell you a secret. My mother was Russian Orthodox. She took us only to her church, so I know all the Russian Orthodox prayers, but only a few Catholic ones." Of course, I did not know any Russian Orthodox prayers, but since part of the population of Bialystok was Russian Orthodox, my story was credible. Miss Bisłowska seemed very pleased to hear it. I could read her thoughts: she was glad I wasn't Jewish. She would much rather deal with a Russian Orthodox girl....*
>
> *Once in her church, I repeated the prayers after the others and mimicked them as best I could.*

Fear of committing a *faux pas* and standing out in some way did not leave my mother for a moment throughout the Sunday service.

With the church outing behind her, Mother was much relieved that she had passed that "test," but nonetheless had a growing sense of unease and yearned to leave Miss Bisłowska's home as soon as possible. The thought that she might bring trouble upon the good woman horrified her. As she wrote in her memoir: *"I came to love that woman. I thought to myself that if I survived the war, I would be very kind to her, better than a daughter would be to her own mother."* Thus, within days of her arrival in Bialystok, primarily in order to avoid jeopardizing Miss Bisłowska, Mother went to the *Arbeitsamt* (employment office) to seek a job which would provide her with another housing option.

The affidavit of previous employment given to her by Hermann Meyer probably saved Mother from hard labor. Instead, she was sent to work as

Chapter Two | Bialystok

a maid for the Majerises, an architect and his wife, who were recent arrivals from Germany. They were an odd couple. The husband, a very reticent man, was 20 years his wife's senior; the wife was loud and bossy, about 28, not that many years older than my mother. The Majerises had no children, and slept in separate rooms. In order to take possession of their beautiful and very spacious apartment on a street re-named by the Germans (called ulica Warszawska before the war), they drove out the family of the rightful owner, a Polish engineer. They had him sent to a labor camp and relegated his wife and three daughters to the attic. Shortly thereafter, they arranged to have them, too, sent to a different labor camp.

Mother's "light" work entailed maintenance of the six-room apartment. She described her responsibilities quite vividly in her unfinished memoir:

> *Working for Mrs. Majeris, I had my hands full all the time. At 6 a.m., I took the ashes out of all the stoves and tossed them in the garden. On my way back, I went to the cellar, filled the buckets with coal, and carried them up. I had to start the fires in all the stoves. I fixed breakfast, then I cleaned all the rooms. Mr. Majeris used one of the rooms as his office. That room had to be ready by 7a.m. I prepared lunch. After lunch, I did the laundry— by hand, of course, using a washboard and boiling the clothes in a huge cauldron, then rinsing everything several times and wringing it by hand. I hung the clothing to dry in the attic and collected it when it was dry. Then there were loads of ironing to do and lots of windows to wash. I also mended clothes and went shopping with Mrs.Majeris to carry the baskets of food. If on some days I finished all of the tasks before 10 p.m., she made me go over peas to pick out wormy ones, or sent me to the cellar to select the slightly rotten potatoes for immediate use. By the end of the day I was so tired that I collapsed into my bed "like a stone" (jak kamień). At 6 a.m. the alarm clock would wake me up again. Day after day, it was work, work, work. And Mrs. Majeris never left the house. She followed me all the time, making sure I didn't rest for a moment. I had my own food stamps, like all the Poles, but she took these away from me. She used all my stamps to buy smoked sausage, which she shipped to her mother in Germany.*

Maria was allowed no breaks; she worked non-stop. Her inevitable visits to the lavatory were barely tolerated and routinely—and within seconds—elicited the yell, "*Was machen sie dort?*" (What are you doing there?).

I have often wondered how humiliating being a maid must have been for my mother, a girl from a respectable Jewish family, whose father had rabbinical training. While always solicitous of her parents, particularly her mother, and familiar with domestic chores, never before had she been required to stoop to such a position of an underling. In fact, during the Soviet occupation, her first job after graduating from a trade high school had been a responsible position as a clerk in a jewelry store.

Mrs. Majeris seemed to derive pleasure from bossing her maid around. Her refrain-like pronouncement "*Maria, Sie sind Pole und Sie muessen das alles machen Was ich Ihnen sage*" (Maria, you are a Pole and you must do everything I tell you) rang in my mother's ears for years after she left Mrs. Majeris's employ. Even when pleased with my mother's work, which she often was, Mrs. Majeris could only offer a back-handed compliment (quite possibly the ultimate praise in her view): "*Sie sind keine Pole; sie sind bestimmt Deutsche*" (You are not a Pole, you must be German). The job was intolerable, yet the one thing Mother appreciated about it was that she did not have to go to church.

The architect's wife undoubtedly had a sadistic streak. The starvation rations of food she allotted her servants were the most striking evidence of this. Mother was chronically hungry. Having taken away my mother's *kartki* (food stamps), to which Mother was fully entitled, Mrs. Majeris allowed her each day only a bowl of soup, some potatoes, and two slices of bread with "growing" marmalade made from beets (that is, marmalade that was self-replicating due to fermentation). Mother was not permitted to touch any other food item. Mrs. Majeris counted each carrot and apple, put markings on sticks of butter, and installed padlocks on all the cupboards, regularly locking them. She watched her supplies with a hawk's eye.

Although perpetually hungry, my mother was afraid to help herself to any food for fear her employer would send her to a camp. Not only did Mrs. Majeris mention such a prospect, by remarking casually that in the camps Poles wore the letter P on the back of their prison garments, but a few days after hiring Mother, she actually did send her gardener, a young Polish boy, to a labor camp for picking an apple from a tree behind the house.

Despite this object lesson, after a few weeks of incessant physical labor Mother's hunger was so overwhelming that, when preparing meals for her employers, she would occasionally scrape some butter from the bottom of the marked cube and swallow it, or place two thin slices of bread in her brassiere, transfer them under the pillow of her bed, and consume them on the sly, usually late at night in the dark. The only thing she could console herself with was that at least her daily portion of soup came from the same pot as the Majerises. The new gardener, Filip, was not so lucky: his soup was cooked from the wormy peas she had to pick through at night. Later, the new gardener was also sent to a camp, allegedly for stealing Mrs. Majeris's rabbit.

In those days, as Mother told me on several occasions, she dreamed of eating a big cutlet and an entire stick of butter after the war. She also recalled vividly one of the happiest moments while in Mrs. Majeris's employ. On that memorable day, Mother was sent to buy groceries alone and had been given the family's food stamps for that purpose. The saleslady forgot to tear off her coupon for baked goods. Mother noticed the error instantly, and returned to the bakery a few minutes later. Using the same coupon, she requested ten additional keiser rolls, all of which she consumed on the way home (a five-minute walk from the bakery)—surprisingly, she did not even suffer from indigestion from them!

Before Christmas, Mother was ordered to clean the whole apartment with particular care. Under Mrs. Majeris's supervision she also cooked up a feast for a dozen expected guests—though of course she was not allowed to taste anything. On Christmas Day, she set the table beautifully, and arranged platters of fish in aspic that she had cooked the day before and assorted other appetizers. Mrs. Majeris was so pleased, that she was moved to do something she never did again—she gave my mother a present, a lightly worn jacket. (Mother suspected it belonged to the evicted lady of the house.)

With the feast fully prepared, Mother was told to stand ready to serve it. After a prolonged wait, it became clear that the guests were not coming. Indeed, not one of the invited guests showed up. Mother served the festive meal to Mrs. Majeris, who was quite out of sorts by then, and her husband, who was reticent as usual. Mother learned subsequently that Mrs. Majeris was rumored to have been a prostitute and was shunned in the German "good society." That was probably the reason behind her guests' snub.

Mrs. Majeris's bossiness and meanness may have stemmed from her feelings of social inferiority. That sense of inferiority may also account for her tendency to put on airs, and her habit of taking my mother along to all her visits at the doctor's office: she wanted to elevate her social status by being seen with a maid. The sole apparent purpose of my mother's presence at the doctor's office was to help Mrs. Majeris take her coat off upon arrival and put it back on when leaving. Of course, given her suspiciousness and watchfulness over her possessions, Mrs. Majeris might have also been reluctant to leave my mother alone in the apartment.

Hardly anyone came to see the Majerises. Their only regular visitor was a Mr. Amer, a Polish architect and former officer of the army who was employed by Mr. Majeris. A man with a sunny disposition, he assisted Mr. Majeris in preparing architectural drafts. His boss kept him quite busy. Assuming that Bialystok would remain in German hands, Majeris expected to own all the houses on the street and was eagerly developing plans for their renovation.

From time to time, Mr. Amer was sent to the kitchen to fetch something. Naturally, he could not help noticing Mrs. Majeris's harsh treatment of her maid. On several occasions he whispered to my mother in Polish, "*Pani musi być żydowką, bo żadna polka by tak ciężko nie pracowała*" (You must be Jewish, because no Polish woman would work so hard).

Indeed, in a matter of a few months Mrs. Majeris brought my mother to a state of exhaustion. Mother wrote in her memoir:

> *From the excessive work from dawn until late at night, from the lack of rest, lack of vitamins, and malnutrition, I felt worse and worse every day. I was growing weaker and weaker, and my legs were constantly swollen. So was my abdomen. I started dropping things inadvertently. I was really afraid I would cause some damage. I had no money to buy replacement items, but I grew so tired nothing mattered to me. One day I plucked up my courage and confessed to Mr. Amer that I was Jewish. He did not want to believe me and thought I was joking. I asked him what I was to do. I knew Mrs. Majeris would not fire me and would not let me leave. His advice was that I go to see a doctor. He thought Mrs. Majeris would have to give me permission to do that. So I told Mrs. Majeris that I could barely walk, that I had chest pains, and I asked her for one hour off to go and see a doctor. She refused and got mad at me.*

My mother's symptoms, particularly the rapidly progressing swelling of her legs, were visible to the naked eye, but Mrs. Majeris ignored them for several days. Mother was so depleted and fatigued she feared she would literally drop dead, so she repeated her request to see a doctor. Mrs. Majeris was furious again, but this time her response was: "Fine! I myself will take you to a doctor, a German doctor, and you'll see that he'll tell you that you must work."

She took Mother to see Doctor Schellenberg, the chief physician in the German (formerly Jewish) hospital in Bialystok. Yet Mrs. Majeris miscalculated. Here is how my mother's remembered the visit:

> *The Chefartzt* [chief physician] *examined me from head to toe in her presence. Then he made me lie down on the gynecological examination table. That was the worst part. I was terribly ashamed to expose myself both before the doctor and Mrs. Majeris. The doctor told her "Sie ist noch Jungfrau"* [She is still a virgin]. *Then he told her I had 200 heartbeats per minute, and "Herzmusklenzindung mit aufsteigene Wasser in die Beine"— an inflammation of the cardiac muscle and retention of water in my legs, and that I had to go to the hospital at once. Otherwise, if the water reached my heart, I would die.*

Contrary to Mrs. Majeris's expectations, Dr. Schellenberg, a father of five and himself not in the best of health (as Mother found out later, half of his left lung had been removed), took pity on the young patient and adhered to medical ethics. Visibly disturbed and disappointed by the doctor's recommendation, Mrs. Majeris used the pretext that Maria needed to collect some of her things before she could check into the hospital, and brought Mother back to the apartment. In her notebook Mother described what followed:

> *We returned home. Mrs. Majeris turned green. She was not sure at whom she should be more angry—me or the doctor. She did not know what to do. If she did not send me to the hospital, I might die. If she did send me, where would she find such a victim as me? Where would she find a maid speaking German and as efficient as I was? I could read her mind, but she told me some of this herself. After a consultation with her husband, she decided that she would let me go to the hospital, but only after I cleaned all the rooms thoroughly, washed all the windows and chandeliers, as well as the doors; and after I did the laundry and all the ironing.*

When my mother finally checked into the hospital, she was swollen and listless for several days. Her symptoms were so severe that on a few occasions Dr. Schellenberg brought medical students to her bed to show them this rare case of such a disease in a young person.

Even in the hospital Mother's nutrition left much to be desired. In the morning she was given two slices of bread with lard, or noodles cooked in milk. As she continued to adhere to the laws of kashrut as much as possible, she could eat none of that, and she routinely gave the bread to other patients. The diets of the German patients at the hospital were much more substantial, but Polish patients were treated to very meager meals, and so Mother's offerings were gladly accepted. For lunch and supper, she was served soup. While the quantities of food were meager, she did not starve, and at least she rested.

Mother felt sick, weak, and lonely. Relatives of the other Polish patients, including the seven women with whom she shared her room, visited frequently, bearing gifts and food. Mother was all alone and could only dream about satisfying her hunger if she survived the war.

The only person who stopped by her room occasionally was Mr. Amer. During his second visit, taking pity on my mother, he suggested that once she was discharged from the hospital she could come to stay with him and his wife. On this occasion, again fearing that she might give herself away because of her ignorance of Christian prayers, Mother asked Mr. Amer to bring her a Catholic prayer book. He complied.

Although Mother learned a few prayers by heart, and Amer also obliged her by teaching her how to cross herself properly, when on one Sunday a nun entered the room and invited the patients to pray, Mom turned red. Her whole face felt aflame. Noticing it, the nun remarked, "You are all red, like a Jewish bastard." Mom promptly assured her that it was her high fever that accounted for the color of her face.

The following Sunday another nun came by. Without even saying good morning, she exclaimed, "Do you see what's going on? God's hand is burning the Jews in the ghetto. Serves them right! That's their punishment for having crucified our Lord." Then the prayers began and everybody sang hymns.

After three weeks, the swelling gradually subsided. Mother was discharged from the hospital. Mrs. Majeris had not visited her even once. Dr. Schellenberg issued Mother a certificate, recommending she be sent to light work, initially for four hours a day at most.

As she had no place to go, and was still quite frail and in need of recuperation, Mother accepted the Amers' offer. They took her in, but almost immediately Mr. Amer began flirting with her blatantly. Mother rebuffed him, remarking that she was surprised he even bothered paying attention to other women, considering how beautiful and smart his wife was. Having overheard this, Mrs. Amer took an instant liking to my mother. She must have perceived her as an ally in her efforts to curb her husband's philandering inclinations. The next day Mrs. Amer slaughtered one of her few chickens and cooked a savory broth. This was truly an extravagance during the war, and a very rare treat for my mother. For several days Mrs. Amer fed Mother well and tried hard to nurse her back to health.

After those few days, although still very weak, Mother was reluctant to impose on the Amers any further. She mobilized herself and early in the morning went to the employment office again. Having read Dr. Schellenberg's note, the clerk at the *Arbeitsamt* grasped her head in exasperation. She kept muttering to herself, "What shall I do now?" The woman was on the horns of a dilemma: Mrs. Majeris had left instructions she wanted my mother back, while Dr. Schellenberg's note explicitly forbade assigning her to physical work.

Probably afraid of the reprisals which Mrs. Majeris was likely to instigate—as the architect's wife was known to send people to camps—the clerk declared that she could not offer Mother a different placement.

Had she not been so weakened by her illness, Mother would probably have returned to Mrs. Majeris's employ, but she realized that the challenges of her former job were simply too daunting—she was physically unable to face them. Mother left the employment office and decided to consult with the Amers about what to do next. To her surprise, shortly after she returned to the Amers' home, Mrs. Majeris appeared there as well. Having found out about Mother's discharge from the hospital and her current whereabouts, she came to plead that Mother return to her employ, promising much better treatment. Mother refused, on the grounds of her poor health.

That afternoon, at the Amers' suggestion, Mother went back to Dr. Schellenberg. His empathy for my mother's plight was obvious, yet he remained silent for quite a while and appeared troubled. (As Mother found out later, his humane and caring attitude toward Polish patients did not sit well with some of the German nuns employed in the hospital. Eventually, they denounced him and had him removed from his post.) Suddenly, he asked my mother, "Can you type?" Having completed a year-long course in typing at a trade school (*gimnazjum kupieckie*), she was in fact very competent as a touch-typist. Dr. Schellenberg asked her to demonstrate her skill, and when she passed the test with flying colors he recommended the hospital hire her.

Mother's duties at the hospital were a far cry from those at the Majerises' home. They involved typing up various documents (case histories, menus for the hospital kitchen, and the like), and quickly expanded to translating for Dr. Schellenberg when he saw his Polish patients. Occasionally she would also assist at the reception desk. She found the hospital and her duties interesting, and her working relationship with Dr. Schellenberg grew increasingly cordial. In no time, Mother learned the essential medical terminology and became a very effective translator and assistant. Indeed, Dr. Schellenberg told her frequently and emphatically, "*Sie mussen ein Arztin sein*" (you must become a doctor). While my mother never realized that dream, she certainly retained a life-long interest in medicine and medical issues.

* * *

Some time before Mother's hospitalization, she had accompanied Mrs. Majeris to the office of Dr. Filipcyk, an SS doctor. While she was sitting in the waiting room, ready to assist Mrs. Majeris in putting her coat on, a side door opened and a slim young girl of 16 or so came out and started rolling out a carpet runner. Initially Mother noticed her tiny hands, but there was something about the girl's looks that made Mother wonder whether she, too, was Jewish. Though the girl had an Aryan-looking face, there was a mixture of fear, suffering, and kindness in her eyes. My mother saw her in the street some days later and whispered, "*Czy Pani jest z ogrodu Allacha?*" (Are you from the garden of Allah?). This was a veiled reference to the ghetto and a "shibboleth" by which Jews on the Aryan side recognized one another. The girl nodded in the affirmative.

A few days later, sent grocery shopping, Mother noticed the girl again, across the street. Maryla, for that was the girl's assumed wartime name, noticed Mother as well. Having crossed the street, she followed my mother until there was no one nearby, so they could talk freely. They exchanged basic information and agreed to coordinate the times they would go on errands. It was during her next encounter with Maryla that Mother learned of three more Jews living in Bialystok outside the ghetto. One of them was my future father, who at that time was using the name Teofil Grol. The others were a woman from Brześć fortunate to have obtained Aryan papers and her less fortunate husband, whom she was hiding in a wardrobe.

Maryla, who like my future father was involved as a courier with a local partisan group, introduced my future parents to each other shortly thereafter, and that's how their Bialystok romance began.

Unbeknownst to my mother, Father had already seen her twice before. After his escape from the Warsaw ghetto, he had briefly visited Brześć, his father's native town, where some of his relatives had still remained. Walking through the Brześć ghetto, he had noticed an attractive girl who was washing a window. As he told my mother later, he was instantly struck by her appearance and thought to himself that it would be worth surviving the war to marry a girl like that. While he'd been very tempted to strike a conversation with her then and there, he had refrained, determined as he was to cross the eastern border of Poland before it was too late. Mother had not noticed him then.

As fate would have it, he had seen her again and listened to her vivid account of conditions in Brześć upon her arrival in the Wysokie Litewskie ghetto. Mother had been addressing a group of people and had not singled him out. However, she remembered her aunt mentioning with much admiration a young man from Warsaw who had given some impassioned speeches in the Wysokie Litewskie ghetto. In the aunt's opinion this fellow (my future father, as Mother later figured it out) was very likely to survive the war because, as the aunt put it in Yiddish, "*Er hot gehat a pysk,*" which roughly translated means that he had the gift of gab. It was in Bialystok that Mother finally did notice my father.

Her recollections of their first meeting always focused on his shabby appearance. Blond, blue-eyed, and very skinny, he wore tennis shoes two sizes too big and tied around his feet with a string, so he would not lose them. His clothing was threadbare, dirty, and torn, and hung on him like on a scarecrow. Lice crawled on his body. In fact, as Mother would tell me, she was quite afraid that Father's appearance might attract the Gestapo's attention, particularly because his long nose contributed to his Semitic look.

Among the first questions my mother asked her future husband was, "What size shoes did you wear before the war?" Equipped with this information, she took it upon herself to secure him a decent pair. The next day, she talked to an old Jew who was regularly brought from the Bialystok ghetto to work in the hospital garden. She offered to pay him if he located a pair of shoes my father's size. A day or two later, the Jew did bring a fairly decent pair to the hospital, but Mother's good intentions almost cost her life. Not seeing Mother at the reception desk where she usually typed, the old Jew asked someone—"Where is the Jewish girl who works here?" While eventually he located Mother and they completed the transaction, she was petrified that he may have blown her cover. In the following few days, each time a co-worker approached her, Mother was convinced she saw suspicious looks.

Shortly afterwards, Dr. Schellenberg left the hospital, denounced by the German nuns. Prior to his departure, he was thoughtful and kind enough to give my mother a supply of medications for her condition (one drug, "woryl," really helped her, and she unsuccessfully looked for it after the war) and arranged for her transfer to another easy job. The new position entailed dusting, repairing, and cataloging books in the municipal library. Access to the library was restricted to German patrons only. Mother was greatly relieved, and celebrated this new job with the Amers, in whose house she continued to live.

* * *

Smitten by Mother and eager to marry her, my future father found out where she lived and started visiting her with increasing frequency. Although Mother's attempts to get him better clothing were gradually crowned with success, she feared that his visits might arouse suspicion and tried to dissuade him from coming. She discouraged him for other reasons as well: to put it bluntly, Mother had serious objections to him on both religious and ideological grounds. Yet Father ignored her frequent rebuffs. (Mother, as she herself told me, would repeatedly say, *"Co się Pan do mnie przyczepił?"*—Why are you pursuing me?, or literally, "Why are you clinging to me?").

My future parents came from very different backgrounds. Born in a provincial town and brought up in a religious, middle-class family proud of its *yiches* (good pedigree), Mother accepted the traditional way of life unconditionally. My father, on the other hand, rebelled against it. His background, his atheism, and his leftist leanings put Mother off. Almost seven years her senior, the son of a poor Warsaw carpenter and a midwife, and a member of the Communist party who had been imprisoned in Bereza Kartuska for his political activities before the war, Father was hardly the ideal candidate for a husband in her eyes. In fact, Mother had been betrothed to a rabbi's son.

Were it not for the war and their accidental encounter in Bialystok, my parents would most likely never have married each other. They represented fundamentally different mentalities, political orientations, and outlooks on life. But the war did bring them together, and my father's pursuit was relentless.

His frequent visits did arouse suspicion among the neighbors. Fearing for themselves as well as for my mother, the Amers thought it best for Mother to move. Mr. Amer arranged for his sister, Mrs. Potapow, who lived in a different part of town, to take Mother in. My father's dogged courtship continued after this move as well. Almost daily, he wrote poems extolling my mother's virtues.[1] He also persuaded her to become involved with the partisan group, which gave him a pretext to see her quite often. Mother

---

[1] Dad kept writing poems to my mother throughout his life. I found in my mother's belongings poems (indeed, peans!) and love letters sent by him when he was away from home, as well as assorted greeting cards. He would often succumb to hyperbole. A card dated March 8, 1993 (fifty years after their marriage!), contained this inscription: *"Mojej żonie, najdroższej Marysi Grol— najbardziej szlachetnej kobiecie pod słońcem—najgorętsze życzenia w Dniu Święta Kobiet składa ubóstwiający mąż, Teofil. Paryż, 8.3.93."* (To my wife, dearest Marysia [diminutive form of Maria] Grol—the most noble woman under the sun—the very best [literally, the hottest] wishes on International Women's Day offered by her adoring husband, Teofil. Paris, March 8, '93.)

obtained medications at the hospital, which were crucial for the wounded or sick partisans, and father would come to pick them up.

Finally, Father prevailed: Mother consented to marry him. Perhaps she was flattered by his courtship. His ardent pursuit and his numerous and passionate poems, expressing in hyperbolic terms his deep love, devotion, and out-and-out admiration may have won her over, or perhaps, seeing his physical frailty and his dire living conditions, Mother was moved by compassion to come to his rescue. Yet, on the eve of their wedding, as Mother revealed to me and my sister years later, she had a very disturbing dream. Her mother appeared in it and pleaded with her in sorrowful tones, using emphatic Yiddish expressions, not to marry Father.

Despite the dream, the wedding did take place the next day, during Passover in 1943. Based on my mother's account, it was an exceedingly modest affair. The bride did not wear an elegant gown: her entire wardrobe in those days consisted of a few well-worn garments. Likewise, the bridegroom was most shabbily dressed. There was no pomp and fanfare of any kind, and not a single relative on either the bride's or the groom's side attended: they were most likely all dead by then. The Brześć ghetto and the Wysokie Litewskie ghetto had been liquidated, and the Warsaw and the Bialystok ghettoes were in their final throes.[2] Only two witnesses were present at the makeshift marriage ceremony: Maryla, the inadvertent matchmaker, and the woman from Brześć, who before the war, as it turned out, had worked at the fabric store owned by Mother's brother-in-law, Malkil Pinczuk. A Jewish doctor in transit through Bialystok officiated.

* * *

My parents started their married life pretending to be a Polish couple. Father moved into my mother's newly-rented room in Mrs. Potapow's house. Mother bought some special toxic liquid in the pharmacy and succeeded in getting rid of the lice that infested both his body and his hair. She nourished him and bought him some decent clothing. He continued writing poetry dedicated to her, continued his collaboration with the partisans, and found a job as a baker's assistant in charge of supplies.

[2] Among my parents' papers I found an invitation to a commemoration of the seventeenth anniversary of the uprising of the Bialystok Ghetto in August 17, 1943.

Most of the clothes Father wore were obtained through Mother's co-workers at the library, Mrs. Wawrzyniak and Mrs. Wąsowicz. The former, the director of the library, was a totally uneducated former maid, sent from Germany to Bialystok as part of the *Einsatz*, that is, the occupation by the Germans of the "regained Eastern territories." Her brother had been killed on the Eastern front, so she was willing to sell Mother his jacket and some shirts. Other items for my father, like socks and a leather belt, were bought through the services of Mrs. Wąsowicz, who was Polish, but who owed her job and her access to the black market to her German lover. A single mother of a teenage son, Mrs. Wąsowicz had taught craftwork before the war and was good at repairing damaged books. Her teenage son, perhaps to ingratiate himself to her lover, spied for the Germans, denouncing Poles who slaughtered pigs for their own consumption, which was in violation of the Germans' regulations.

Employment in the library was most desirable during the war years. Dr. Schellenberg must have used considerable pull to secure the position for my mother. Her co-workers, however, accepted Mother reluctantly. As they admitted openly, they would much rather have seen a friend of theirs obtain the job. Of the two, Mrs. Wawrzyniak was more inclined to tolerate my mother's presence in the library. Ignorant, and unable to spell or type, she found Mother a convenient underling to whom she could relegate most of her responsibilities. Mrs. Wąsowicz, on the other hand, strenuously attempted to get rid of the new employee. She may have been instigated to do so by Mrs. Majeris, whom she knew and who, most likely, was quite annoyed by my mother's escape from her despotic employ.

Thus, on one occasion, Mrs. Wąsowicz sent Mother to deliver library books to a certain address. As Mother was leaving, she told her, "Don't take any ID with you." Mother was rather puzzled by that remark, but could not grasp the motive behind it. She left, located the appropriate office building, entered into the vestibule, and asked to see the person for whom the books were intended. Told the man was busy, she was asked to sit down and wait on a side bench. As she waited patiently for close to an hour, she could see through the window as hundreds of Gypsies were herded into the back yard. More and more were led in. She could hear their screaming and wailing.

While she was waiting, the male receptionist struck up a conversation with Mother and offered to sell her a pair of man's gloves. Mother expressed interest, saying she might consider buying them for her husband. Shown two left gloves, she declined, but asked the man if he had other items of men's clothing for sale. No, he replied, yet he could sell her a nice dress, he said. The receptionist went to the back room and returned with a beautiful red dress exactly my mother's size. Mother was speechless for a long while, and not because she was looking at an incredibly lovely garment, which was a rare find during the war, but, as she told me, because the night before she had had a dream in which her mother had told her, "*Mashele, ich vel dir koyfn a sheynem roytn kleyd*" (My dear Masha, I will buy you a nice red dress). Mother bought the dress, and it was a treasured possession of hers for many years to come.

The man to whom Mother was ordered to deliver the books showed up at long last. He was wearing an SS uniform, and asked Mother to follow him to his office. Asked to sit down and wait while he stepped out, Mother obliged. He returned momentarily with an older Gypsy woman. The woman started talking, raising her voice and gesticulating in a more and more agitated manner. The SS-man watched Mother closely and kept asking what the Gypsy woman was saying. Mother repeatedly declared that she did not understand. He could see from her demeanor that she was telling the truth, and the SS man let Mother go.

The errand was obviously a ploy. Mrs. Wąsowicz must have learned from her German lover about the planned roundup of the Gypsies and had hoped to include Mother in their transport to an extermination camp. Her plan backfired. My Mother escaped with her life—and gained a new dress.

Other efforts by Mrs. Wąsowicz to get rid of my mother amounted to more innocuous, but annoying, vexations. Once, she offered my mother a coupon valid for lunch at a dining hall serving meals exclusively to Germans. Reluctant to refuse her co-worker and routinely hungry, Mother went there during her lunch break. Feeling rather apprehensive in that environment, she ordered some soup, found an available table, and without looking at her dish sat down to consume it. She put one spoonful of the soup in her mouth and spat it out in disgust. The kitchen personnel, who were watching her from a distance, were splitting their sides with laughter, clearly having fun at her expense. Not only was the soup extremely salty, but black bugs covered its surface. Mrs. Wąsowicz had conspired with the women working in the kitchen and marked the coupon. Needless to say, Mother never went to that dining hall, never accepted Mrs. Wąsowicz's "gifts," and tried not to go out during her lunch breaks after that incident.

One day, my future father came to the library. Mrs. Wąsowicz, an outspoken antisemite and German sympathizer, examined him closely. After his departure, she commented loudly that he had the face of Mephistopheles. Fearing that this was a veiled reference to his Semitic looks, Mother quickly interjected that he came from a good family and had a brother who was a priest.

There were good reasons to assume a defensive posture in Mrs. Wąsowicz's presence. She was a *Volksdeutsch*—an "ethnic" German— and would not hesitate to denounce a Jew, as she had demonstrated very effectively on various occasions. Once, when a neighbor stopped by and reported that an escapee from the Bialystok ghetto came to her apartment, took some bread, and was hiding in the bathroom downstairs, Mrs. Wąsowicz instantly rushed downstairs, intent on catching the Jew and delivering him to the Gestapo. The emaciated Jew ran out of the bathroom, but she chased him, managed to catch up with him in the street, and holding fast to his arm yelled for someone to arrest him. None of the passersby responded at first. Ultimately, she talked some German into turning him in.

* * *

My parents lived in a state of constant alertness and fear. For a Jew, just walking the streets of Bialystok was fraught with danger. A man who lived next to the library had a habit of sitting in front of his door, and would repeat a rather unusual greeting each time my mother passed by: "*Dzień dobry pół ryża kobieto*" (Good morning, woman with half-red hair). Although my mother bleached her hair during the war, she was not a redhead. Each time she heard his greeting, therefore, she wondered if he had recognized she was Jewish. That neighbor turned out to be harmless, but Mother had other encounters in the streets that could have ended tragically.

One day, after work, she was waiting at a street corner, where Father was supposed to meet her. A Ukrainian policeman approached her and asked where she lived. She gave him a false address and tried to get away, petrified that my father would appear any moment. Given his Semitic looks, she feared he might be arrested. Mother started walking faster and faster. The policeman followed, yelling, "Zydówka! żydówka!" (A Jew! A Jew!). There was instant commotion. A boy riding a bike stopped and joined the crowd of onlookers. Somehow Mother had the presence of mind to yell back at the Ukrainian, "How dare you insult me like that! If you weren't wearing a German uniform, I would deal with you differently!" Her improvised performance must have been credible enough, because the crowd dispersed.

On another occasion, as she was approaching the house where she lived, a Polish man from Brześć recognized Mother, addressed her by her real name, Masza Pinczuk, and insisted he knew her. She told him that he was mistaken; she had never even been to Brześć. Undeterred by Mother's denials, he followed her. She ducked into a store, but he was waiting outside when she came out. Remembering her father's tale of his survival during World War I (he ran off and hid in an outhouse, and thus stayed alive while the rest of his battalion died), she followed his example, dashed behind the building, and hid in an outhouse. Three hours later, she emerged cautiously, still very frightened and tense, went home, and urgently asked her landlady if anyone had come to ask for her. Fortunately, she found, she had succeeded to evade the man from Brześć.

Yet another potentially dangerous incident involved Mother's refusal to allow a German to use her rented room for card games. The man remembered her from the time she had worked in the kitchen of the Wysokie Litewskie police station, and approached her with a "business proposal." He had the idea that he would invite his buddies into her room for card games, would swindle them, and would share the profits with my mother. Mother refused not only on moral grounds, but out of fear that he would bump into my father. The man threatened her, and made her very anxious. When he approached her a second time and started pressuring her, she used an interesting excuse: she told him she was engaged to a German officer who would not tolerate the visits of other men. At Mom's request the next door neighbor, who happened to be standing by, confirmed that a German officer did come to visit my Mother. Indeed, this was shortly after, Herman Meyer had visited Bialystok, located Mother at her new address, and stopped by to return to her the gold watch she had slipped into his pocket at the Majeris's apartment. (The gold watch he returned to my mother is still in my possession; I treasure it immensely. It is my only family heirloom and the only object I own which was touched by my maternal grandmother, who—like my many other murdered relatives—I was never fortunate enough to know.)

Father had numerous brushes with death as well: his partisan activities contributed to both his and my mother's sense of vulnerability. Occasionally he stored weapons obtained illegally. More often, he produced anti-Nazi leaflets and distributed them. A search of my parents' room would inevitably have meant their end. Yet, miraculously, my parents survived the war under their assumed identities and were liberated by the Soviet Army. When I learned about the extent and ferocity of the hunt for Jews, about the Jedwabne affair and the similar murders of Jews in the Bialystok region, my parents' survival struck me as even more miraculous than it had appeared to me previously.[3]

By the time the Soviets entered Bialystok, my parents were well prepared for their arrival. Informed by the partisans about the approaching front, Father, ably assisted by Mother, had dyed some sheets red to turn them into Soviet flags and had produced banners welcoming the Soviet liberators. The group of people who came out with my parents into the streets of Bialystok to welcome the Soviet Army was very small, but they greeted the liberators with gusto. Jubilant, they waved the red flags, carried the prepared slogan in Russian (*Да здравствует советская армия!*— Long Live the Soviet Army!), and kissed and hugged the Soviet soldiers, ecstatic that liberation had come at long last.

My mother remembered that day in great detail her whole life, and could even quote the songs sung by the Soviet soldiers. She jumped for joy then, and was even filmed by a news team accompanying the entry of the Soviet army. I hope to find that footage some day in either Russian or Polish archives. It would have special value to me, and not only because it would show me my young parents—it would also show me my own "pre-history,"

---

[3] See Antony Polonsky and Joanna B. Michlic, eds., *The Neighbors Respond: The Controversy over the Jedwabne Massacre in Poland* (Princeton: Princeton University Press, 2004). In addition to the now notorious Jedwabne murders, information about other atrocities in nearby towns and villages has been confirmed. For example, Radosław Ignatiew, the prosecutor from the Bialystok office of the Institute of National Memory (Instytut Pamięci Narodowej), finally confirmed (71 years after the crimes were committed!) that in August of 1941 women from the Szczuczyn ghetto (near Bialystok) were brought out to work on Polish farms in the villages of Szczuczyn and Bzury (and possibly others), then murdered with scythes and hoes and buried in the fields after they had completed their tasks. This was free labor for the farmers—the women worked in the hope of obtaining some potatoes or other food. According to the testimony of a local witness, the Jewish women were murdered by drunken Polish men. (Agnieszka Domanowska, "Bili kosami i motykami," *Gazeta Wyborcza*, June 15, 2012).

for I had been conceived in Bialystok and my mother was pregnant with me on July 25, 1944, the day of the liberation.

My mother and father

in 1945

in 1946

in 1946

The exuberance was short-lived. Mother told me how the Soviet soldiers' triumphant march was interrupted by a German bombardment; how the welcoming group dispersed instantly; and how suddenly my parents, still carrying the slogans and flags, found themselves practically alone in the streets. When they tried ducking into nearby homes, no one would let them in. They ran in the streets as the bombs were raining. Finally, my mother's ardent pleas to let them in because she was pregnant won them admission into a crowded cellar where everyone was muttering Catholic prayers and my parents feared their silence might give them away. My mother divulged to me that as she crouched in that cellar, silently and in her own words praying in Yiddish to survive the bombardment, she thought to herself that, given the circumstances during her pregnancy and the "secondary stress" her fetus was experiencing, the child she was carrying in her womb would be either an idiot or a genius. Blinded by her love for me, all my life she told me I was the latter.

Chapter Three

From Bialystok to Dubno

Late one cold, wintry night a couple was trudging in deep snow. Gusts of wind were chilling their bodies. Unfamiliar with their surroundings, the couple strenuously looked for signs of human activity. Yet, given the hour, it is unsurprising that no one was out. Emaciated and tense, they were plodding in virtual darkness.

* * *

A few months earlier, penniless and exhausted, the couple had reached the small Ukrainian town of Dubno in the province of Volhynia. Hoping to put the horrors of war behind them, they had left Bialystok and headed east, walking, occasionally getting rides on peasants' wagons, and, mostly, hitchhiking on Soviet military trucks. The aroma of boiling potatoes as they passed peasants' houses made their hunger more acute. When they begged for food, they were repeatedly turned away.

On one occasion, the woman, pregnant, pleaded with a 5-year-old boy they passed to give her the slice of bread he was eating. He generously did so. She quickly consumed the bread, but could not hold it down; it was too much of a shock to her digestive system. She regretted very much not being able to absorb the rare gift she had received and give nourishment to her fetus.

In Dubno, the couple managed to find a family willing to take them in. The tiny room they rented was actually a bathroom from which the bathtub had been removed so that a mattress could be placed on the floor. Cut pieces of a tree trunk served as their table and chairs. That was the sum total of their furniture.

* * *

They were out now, marching in the snow, because the woman had gone into labor in the middle of the night. Her water had broken and contractions had begun. Panicked, she had asked her husband to find a doctor. Although his mother had been a midwife before the war, the husband had appeared ignorant of the urgency of the situation and had suggested waiting until morning, but his young wife made it clear she could not delay the arrival of the baby.

The husband got dressed hastily and ventured out in search of a doctor. He succeeded in locating one relatively quickly, but this did not resolve the problem. Upon arrival at the couple's "abode," the doctor took one look around himself and declared the quarters unsuitable for the delivery of a child. He gave the couple the address of a *rod-dom* (род-дом), a small clinic where babies were delivered. It was located only a kilometer away, he assured them, and then departed to his other business.

The couple had no choice but to bundle up and hike through the knee-deep snow to find the clinic. The town was asleep. There were no street signs and no one around to ask for directions. The woman's birth pangs continued, increasing in intensity. Miraculously, they found the building at around 3 a.m.

An elderly *babushka* (granny), the sole custodian as it turned out, let them in. She ushered the pregnant woman into a freezing room and ran off to wake up the obstetrician in a nearby house.

Shivering from the cold and barely able to tolerate the increasing intensity of her labor pangs, the woman grew more and more anxious. Her husband was not allowed into the shabby delivery room. When the *babushka* returned some time later and began to start a fire in the stove, the pregnant woman, starved for human warmth, pleaded with the granny to postpone the task and just place a hand on her face.

Luckily, the obstetrician arrived in time to deliver a healthy baby girl at around 8 a.m. The baby came into the world with a loud cry. The date was January 19, 1945—four months before the end of World War II.

Only hours after the baby's birth, the husband and the young mother, carrying the baby swaddled in some rags, were trudging through the snow again. As they were approaching the house where they had rented their room, they saw an agitated neighbor running toward them. She was yelling,

Chapter Three | From Bialystok to Dubno

"*Pani Marysiu! Pani Marysiu! Warszawa wyzwolona!*" (Ms. Marysia [a diminutive form of Maria]! Ms. Marysia! Warsaw has been liberated!). In fact, the Red Army had marched into Warsaw on January 17, 1945, and that date had been declared the day of liberation, but the news had not reached Dubno until two days later.

The baby, of course, was *moi même*, and the young couple was my parents: my mother, née Masza Pinczuk, aged 23 at the time, and my father Teofil (Tovyeh) Grol, aged 30. My parents took the news of Warsaw's liberation as a wonderful omen, a portent of a new beginning for them and a happy life for me. This is the story of my birth, as it was told to me on various occasions by my parents.

* * *

To state that my parents' challenges and emotional burdens were horrendous when I was born would be a major understatement. The reality they had to confront was daunting. Being Jewish in a provincial Ukrainian town was still fraught with risks in the final months of the war, and even upon its conclusion. Moreover, my parents were essentially penniless. There were also the more mundane practical challenges: for example, upon entering the bathroom which constituted their home, my parents had to resolve their first dilemma. Should they cut up the only sheet they owned into diapers, or preserve it so they would have something to sleep on? Local factories had not produced anything for several years, and the stores were empty, so obtaining any household items was most difficult. It would be next to impossible to find diapers. What were they to do? My mother's ingenuity came to the fore then, as it had before and continued to do on many other occasions. She sent my father on a special mission to buy *onuce* from the Soviet soldiers. My father did not even know until later that day the Russian equivalent of this Polish word. *Onuce*, or *portyanki* in Russian, were the square pieces of cloth, which, in the absence of socks, Soviet soldiers were issued to wrap around their feet. Malnourished, a number of soldiers willingly parted with such personal belongings in exchange for food or money, and a few hours later Father returned triumphantly with several foot bindings. I have no idea what he bartered to obtain them, but they saved the day—and many subsequent ones—by serving as my diapers. Another "trophy" my father managed to obtain some days later was a wooden cradle with one of its rockers broken. It, too, served me well after it was fixed.

I have tried to imagine the bathroom that was my home for the first months of my life. I was too little then, of course, to have any recollection of it now. Yet, occasionally, throughout my life, most often in the shower, as my eyes are closed and the water streams down my face, I see a black-and-white pattern of squares resembling the tiled walls of a bathroom. I wonder sometimes whether that is an early visual memory imprinted on my subconscious mind.

* * *

As my mother would later tell me repeatedly, Father was ecstatic when I was born. He sang to me, recited poetry to me, pampered me in every conceivable way. Long before I was capable of eating solids, he tried to feed me a hard boiled egg, a treat and a luxury in those days. Fortunately, my mother saved me from choking when he alerted her that I was holding my head in an unusual way.

Father would swell with pride when I was complimented on my looks, for until I turned into a skinny, gap-toothed girl at the age of seven, I happened to be a pretty child with big blue eyes and wavy blond hair. Not only was he proud to be a father, but naturally given to hyperbolic rhetoric he freely expressed his view that my birth was a triumph. He perceived it as symbolic: as a victory of life over death, of good over evil; as a compensation for the losses and pains inflicted on my parents during the war.

My birth was indeed a miracle, and not just in the conventional sense that every healthy birth is miraculous. The odds of my being born, even the odds of my parents surviving the war, were minimal. Of the 30,000 members of the Jewish community of Brześć, my mother was one of very few who survived—her estimate was that there were about a dozen of them. She evaded the "liquidation" of three ghettoes, that of Brześć (Brest), Wysokie Litewskie, and Bialystok. The rest of her family of about 70 people perished without a trace. My father's entire family in Warsaw was murdered as well: his mother, his younger brother, and other relatives. Father escaped from the ghettoes of Warsaw, Kovel, Brześć, and Wysokie Litewskie, and managed to avoid being taken into the Bialystok ghetto. Had my parents not succeeded in all of their escapes, I would have been one of the millions of phantom, unborn Jewish children whose parents perished in the Holocaust. That thought has crossed my mind repeatedly throughout my adult life. Reading memoirs of those who were children during the Holocaust has also made me aware of the difference being born just a few years later made in my life.[1]

After reading books about the Holocaust, or viewing films like Lantzman's "Shoah" or Spielberg's "Schindler's List," I would emerge with a tremendous sense of appreciation for having been born, but also with a sense of profound admiration for my parents, who despite their wartime experiences had shown their indomitable spirit by bouncing back from their many adversities, completing their higher educations, making friends, creating a close knit family, and surrounding me with affection, warmth, and love. I admire to this day their resilience and irrepressible drive to make the most of their lives.

Many Holocaust survivors are reluctant to tell their children about their war-time experiences. A few years ago, a social worker, a Gentile woman employed by a Jewish nursing home in Toronto, confided to me that she had been repeatedly told horror stories by the elderly Holocaust survivors residing in that home. When asked if they had shared these stories with their children, the standard answer they gave her was that they had not. The reasons for their reluctance can be guessed—primarily an unwillingness to burden their children. But I received yet another very explicit and poignant clarification from Dr. Felix Milgrom, professor of epidemiology at the University of Buffalo, of blessed memory. He shared with me his story, that he was hidden in a cellar for many months, along with his wife Halina, and told me he had written about his wartime experiences. When I asked him if he had shown his memoir to his two sons, his response was a rhetorical question: "Do you think a woman who was raped would tell her children about it?" His reply made it abundantly clear to me how hard—even shameful—it was to admit to the abuse and humiliation survivors had suffered.

Yet my parents, and particularly my mother, were not reticent. They were willing to share with me the details of their survival. Perhaps their

---

[1] Some of these volumes were Irena Grudzinska-Gross and Jan Tomasz Gross, eds., *War Through Children's Eyes* (Stanford, CA: Hoover Institution Press, 1985), and Kaja Finkler and Golda Finkler, *Lives Lived and Lost* (Boston: Academic Studies Press, 2012).

experiences were less drastic than the experiences of those in labor and concentration camps. Perhaps to some extent they were proud of their quick wits and resourcefulness. And, luckily, my parents were spared situations which would have forced them to engage in unethical behavior—that is, crimes or betrayals. Perhaps their vicissitudes were less humiliating.

Their stories are my legacy. Yet it is not an easy legacy…

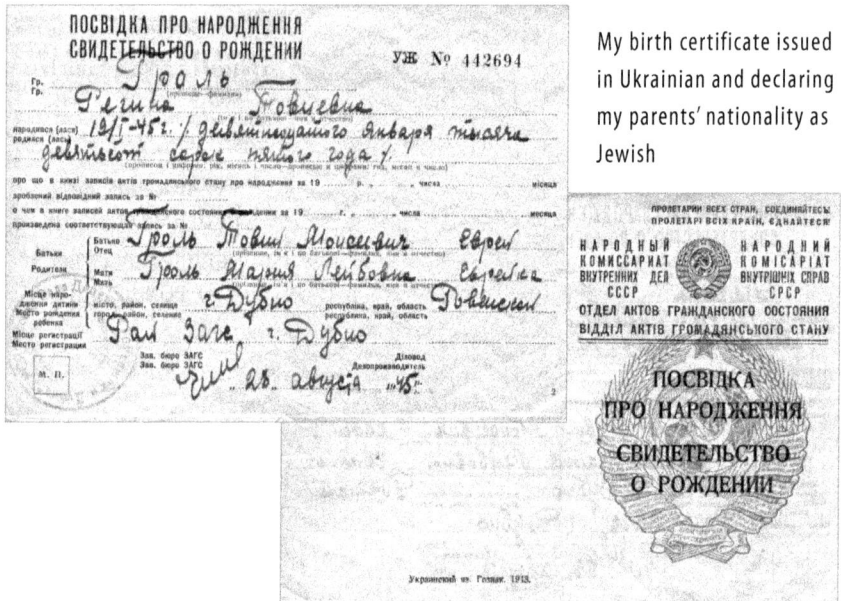

My birth certificate issued in Ukrainian and declaring my parents' nationality as Jewish

My parents and me in Dubno, 1945

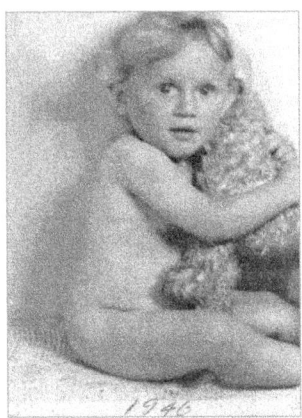

My picture taken upon our return to Poland

Father and me, 1945

Mother and me, 1946

Chapter Four

Further Migrations: From Dubno to Katowice to Haifa

My parents left Dubno and returned to Poland in 1946. Initially, my father was reluctant to do so, and wavered. The Soviet Union, which now included both Eastern and Western Ukraine, was a land of promise. Minority groups were officially guaranteed equal rights, and Father assumed that he would no longer be stigmatized as a Jew.

Although he truly missed his native city of Warsaw, and Polish culture was very close to his heart, he knew that Poland had become a massive Jewish cemetery and had been a country of persistent antisemitism even before the war. He had painful memories of having to sit in a corner, on the benches specifically designated for the few Jews allowed to study at Warsaw University under the *numerus clausus* policy. Likewise, the wartime indifference of his Polish compatriots to the plight of the Jews, and the frequent denunciations, were fresh on his mind. The Soviet Union, on the other hand, promised equality, access to education, and employment. Indeed, a few years earlier, under the Soviet occupation, he had already been given the opportunity to work at a profession he liked—he had been a teacher in Luck and then principal of a high school in the town of Kovel in Ukraine. Father yearned to return to that high school. However, other survivors' warnings that the Ukrainians were still "hunting" for Jews and did not refrain from killing them kept my father from going back.

Hopeful promises were also made by the Soviet-backed provisional Polish government. On July 22, 1944, the Polish Committee of National Liberation issued the July Manifesto (*Manifest lipcowy PKWN*), which included the following statement: "*Zydom po bestialsku tępionym przez *okupanta zapewniona zostanie [...] odbudowa ich egzystencji oraz prawne i faktyczne równouprawnienie*" (Jews bestially exterminated by the occupier will be assured [...] of the rebuilding of their existence and of legal as well as factual equality).[1] My father either did not know about this document or simply had more confidence in the Soviet regime than the Polish one.

In 1945, when Poland's borders were moved west and the repatriation of Polish citizens became possible, my father resisted the idea of leaving Dubno. Twice my mother submitted applications for repatriation on behalf of the family; twice my father withdrew them. Finally, with much effort, Mother succeeded in persuading him that the Soviet Union was not a place to stay. While Father was an idealist, and remained one for the rest of his life, my mother was much more down to earth and always had a great deal of common sense. She prevailed using another powerful argument—she was determined to go back to Poland in the hope of finding any relatives who might still be alive.

When during the return trip she did stop in Brześć, by then a border town (her family home was now located in Soviet Belarus), she learned that her entire family had perished. One eyewitness gave her a detailed account of how her father had been dragged out of the bunker and shot in the back yard in plain view. As she told me on several occasions, other than the emotional pain and the feeling of survivor's guilt, the only "benefit" Mother derived from her one and only postwar visit to her native town was the confirmation of her family's good name. Some strangers now occupied Mother's house, and they repeated to her what they had been told, "*Tu mieszkali porządni ludzie*" (Decent people lived here). These words meant a great deal to my Mother. They were her precious legacy.

At the time my parents arrived in Poland, returnees had to build their new lives on their own, not supported by the special government programs for repatriating Polish citizens. As Warsaw had been repeatedly bombed and essentially razed, no housing was available there. My parents were advised to go to Poland's newly acquired western territory, and managed to get a ride to the town of Bytom in the region of Silesia. It was already getting dark when the driver dropped them off in a street they were completely unfamiliar with. They knew no one in the town.

---

[1] *Manifest Lipcowy PKWN. Deklaracja PPR* (Warszawa, 1982),13.

After many inquiries, my parents, with me in my mother's arms, were directed to a dilapidated school building where a huge room had been converted into sleeping quarters for displaced and homeless people.

During that very first night, my father squashed a mouse in his sleep. Anxious that mice might attack me, or, as we all slept on the floor, get into my infant mouth and make me choke, Father went to the authorities pleading for some better lodgings. Being the persuasive man that he was, within days he secured an apartment in Bytom at 18 Mickiewicza Street. Some time later we moved to Katowice, the capital of Silesia, and obtained an apartment at 18 Opolska Street. It was in that second apartment, according to my mother, that I took my first steps. I was standing next to a chair, holding it, and suddenly released my grip and started my march into the future.

Father obtained a job in the Jewish ORT (Organization for Rehabilitation and Training) school and later taught in the three colleges in Katowice—the College for Economics (*Wyższa Szkoła Ekonomiczna*), the College for Music (*Wyższa Szkoła Muzyczna*), and the College for Arts (*Wyższa Szkoła Plastyczna*). It was in Katowice—or strictly speaking, in a hospital in the suburb of Gliwice, that my sister Halina was born, on February 12, 1949.

Injected with several vaccinations immediately after her birth, my sister got very sick. As a result of either a toxic overdose or some side effects, she developed a high fever and symptoms of dehydration. Yet the hospital released her after a few days, most likely to minimize its mortality rates.

I recall distinctly my parents' heroic fight for my baby sister's life. They arranged for house calls by private doctors and regular visits by nurses. I still remember the enormous needles used to hydrate her, the many consultations with physicians, the pleas for medications and help. For 24 hours a day my mother watched over my sister, hardly ever leaving her bedside. Fortunately, my sister recovered fully and was blessed with relatively good health for most of her life.

As an only and adored child until then, I suddenly felt neglected when all of this attention was showered on my sister. I clearly recall an instance of sibling rivalry: on one occasion, feeling ignored, I climbed into my sister's baby carriage, with my legs protruding, and repeatedly screamed: "*Ja jestem Halinka*" (I am Halinka—a diminutive form of Halina). This incident became part of our family lore.

Chapter Four | Further Migrations: From Dubno to Katowice to Haifa

The author on the far right at a Jewish preschool in Katowice

Apparently, I was not an easy child for the following few years. Later in my life, my mother was very contrite about having often resorted to spanking. She apologized, saying that these were the commonly accepted norms then. In fact, she had followed the doctor's advice: my pediatrician, Dr. Sas, clearly condoned physical punishment. His philosophy regarding dealing with unruly children was, "*Do 10-ciu lat proszę mówić do dolnej głowy, a od 10-ciu lat do górnej głowy*" (Talk to the lower head until the age of ten, and to the upper head after the age of ten).

In my case, the spanking actually ended earlier. When Mother asked me what gift I would like for my eighth birthday, I replied that I wanted none. Instead, I requested that she stop spanking me. She promised to respect my wish and kept her word: there was no spanking ever after. I still marvel at my early assertiveness and negotiation skills.

* * *

Our family's situation was gradually improving. My mother completed a special college program for teachers of Russian and began teaching the language to groups of adults. I attended a Jewish kindergarten in Katowice. Father was advancing professionally, and we moved to a better apartment in the suburb of Brynów.

Ostensibly, this was progress and an improvement of our situation, but I do recall some disturbing moments. We were imposed as tenants by the Communist authorities on the owner of a private villa in Brynów. The owner and his family lived on the first floor, while we received the second floor apartment. We were allowed no access to the garden. Once, playing with my sister, I tossed a ball quite far and had to venture into the garden to retrieve it. The landlord scolded me harshly. At seven years old, my sense of legal entitlements or prohibitions was probably limited, but he totally overlooked my age. I do remember feeling apprehensive about any contact with him, and my parents sensed that.

Another incident disturbed them even more than my anxiety about our living situation. I attended a public elementary school in Brynów. While my looks did not make me stand out, I was the only child who had no uncles, aunts, or grandparents, which surprised my classmates, most of whom came from big Catholic families. My best friend then, Trudzia, was one of eleven children. I was also the only child not taking the after-school catechism classes. On a lovely spring day, as I was walking home from school, I was suddenly shoved off the sidewalk and pushed down a slope. I landed in a muddy ditch. The boy who had snuck up behind me and pushed me was a classmate. He followed me into the ditch, stepped on my neck, and called me a kike, and the expression on his face was very mean. While he did no permanent damage to my neck, it hurt for hours.

My face and hands filthy, my clothes muddy, I made it home, still sobbing. It took my mother a long time to calm me down. As I was telling her what had occurred, I could sense her apprehension. That night, I was officially informed by my parents that I was Jewish and that some people did not like Jews. The next day, my father went to see the school principal and reported the incident. He also started exploring relocation. Some time later, we moved to our last Katowice apartment, at 8 Generała Zajączka Street. This time we lived in a lovely little house surrounded by a garden.

I have vivid memories of the years spent in Katowice. The school I was transferred to (TPD #1) was much better than the suburban one, and there were no religion classes offered on its premises. While I was a good student and had excellent rapport with the teachers, the children's biases did not disappear altogether: they still took catechism classes at their churches and I did not. When we played team sports at school and

Chapter Four | Further Migrations: From Dubno to Katowice to Haifa

the captain of the team had to select players, I was usually the last to be selected. This treatment was not related to my physical abilities, as I was quite athletic then.

Still, I do recall fondly some extracurricular activities. Mother signed me up for a children's drama club at the local community center (*Dom kultury*). I enjoyed taking part in performances and was very proud as a ten-year-old to be invited to participate in a radio show which was then transmitted nationally.

My parents also had a routine of taking me and my sister for Sunday morning walks in the park, which were enjoyable, as were our various trips to the countryside. The departures from the city were an attempt to escape the pervasive dust and soot there. Silesia was full of coal mines and steel mills. In the postwar industrialization fervor, the region was being developed without any consideration of the harmful effects on the environment or the inhabitants. There was soot everywhere in Katowice. My school uniform consisted of a navy blue frock with a white collar. I would leave for school in the morning with a clean white collar, but by the time I returned home, both the collar and my face were grey because of the soot in the air.

A big industrial city, Katowice was also a significant cultural center. It had several colleges, a good philharmonic, and decent theaters. Even foreign artists were invited. I recall my parents taking me to see Gershwin's "Porgy and Bess" in the early fifties. I still remember what a great impression that performance by a touring US company made on me. It may also have been the first time I had seen dark-skinned people.

There are other memories I have retained from that period. I recall the national mourning when Stalin died on March 5, 1953. We had a special assembly at school with speeches and poems extolling Stalin's virtues. I was only eight years old then, but I knew very well who he was even prior to the assembly: the "cult of personality" was pervasive in Poland. Stalin's pictures decorated our school, were seen on posters and placards during various manifestations, as were the pictures of Marx, Engels, and Lenin. Children were indoctrinated even in kindergarten, and had to learn poems in Polish and Russian praising the "leaders." I still remember one kindergarten poem, which rhymes in Russian. Its literal translation would be: "I am a little girl. I play and sing. I have never seen Stalin, but I love him."

> Я маленькая девочка,
> Играю и пою.
> Я Сталина не видела,
> *но я его люблю.*

While I was obviously too young to fully grasp the meaning of the political debates at the time, I do recall the many discussions in our house following Nikita Khrushchev's speech in which he denounced Stalin's purges, the speech he delivered at the 20th Congress of the Communist Party of the Soviet Union. That speech was a trigger for a political liberalization in Poland in 1956. The iron curtain lifted temporarily, and Polish Jews were given permission to leave for Israel. A massive wave of emigration began, and my family joined it in the spring of 1957.

Like most of their friends and acquaintances who had decided to emigrate, my parents ordered a huge wooden box (*lift*) to ship our belongings to Israel. The box was packed with many possessions, such as warm coats and eiderdown bed covers, that turned out to be useless in the hot Israeli climate. Nor did we have much use in Israel for the alleged "treasures," our heavy crystal vases.

* * *

After a brief stay in Vienna, we travelled to Italy by train and, in Genoa, embarked on a boat that took us to Israel.

I still have vivid memories of this Mediterranean voyage. It was my first experience of travel by sea, so the memories are both negative and positive. Among the former type of memories are the sea sickness of the many passengers and my own culinary surprises. Invited to the captain's table, I picked up some black olives from a big platter, assuming they were little plums. I found the taste of this unfamiliar food revolting, salty rather than sweet as I had expected, but I did not want to embarrass my parents by spitting the olives out. It was an agonizing moment. On the positive side, the trip was quite an adventure for my sister and me. I recall the lovely view of Mount Carmel as we were approaching Haifa and the nice welcome we received at the port. However, soon afterwards all of us experienced a shock.

Chapter Four | Further Migrations: From Dubno to Katowice to Haifa

We were sent by bus to a *maabara*, a hastily-built immigrant absorption camp, near the town of Afula. Many such settlements were set up all over Israel in the 1950s to accommodate the massive influx of Jewish refugees from Arab countries as well as immigrants from Eastern Europe.

To this day, whenever I read about or see TV coverage of refugee camps, I have a sinking feeling and a sense of overwhelming empathy for the displaced. I know that this reaction is related to my personal experience, those few days I spent in the *maabarah* near Afula in the spring of 1957. Coming directly from big European cities to this colony of tiny cabins (*tsrifim*) with corrugated metal roofs was a true shock for me and my sister, but especially for my parents. This was not how they had imagined their first home in Israel. There was no running water in the cabins; the closest source of water, a primitive pump shared by several families, was about 300 yards away. We were given buckets to carry the water back to our cabins. The outhouses were also at a considerable distance. The *maabarah* was located in a barren field with hardly any greenery around us. Using the blankets, the few plates, and the kitchen utensils we had been given, my family attempted to function in these austere conditions, yet we could not adjust to them. The desert-like landscape and the sounds of animals at night terrified me.

The next day, my father demanded that we be moved to a different location. Somehow, he had found out that *akademiyim*, that is, people with higher education, were entitled to housing in better absorption centers. My parents qualified. Three days later, assertive man that he was, Father succeeded in getting us transferred to Kiriat Binyamin in the vicinity of Haifa. The absorption colony there was considerably more luxurious than the first. Our cabin was bigger and had indoor plumbing. However, the cabins were built out of asbestos. We learned only years later of the carcinogenic effect.

I started attending summer Hebrew courses for immigrant children as soon as we arrived in Kiriat Binyamin. Since my parents were also busy learning Hebrew and looking for jobs and opportunities to move out of the absorption center to start a normal life, at the ripe old age of twelve I was assigned the role of the family's cook. I learned how to prepare assorted dishes and was actually flattered by my new role.

Six months after our arrival, we moved to our first *shikun*, that is, a normal apartment in Kiriat Eliezer, a suburb of Haifa located at the foot of Mount Carmel. While our apartment was on the fourth floor and there was no elevator, my parents were overjoyed, and so was I. We had a lovely view of the *tayelet* (the promenade) and the sports stadium. My sister, who was eight years old at the time, immediately made friends with all the neighborhood cats and dogs. She also "adopted" some baby rats, bringing them food regularly. We did not know then that she was giving us hints of her future choice of profession. Years later, she became a veterinarian.

The neighborhood of Kiriat Eliezer was dominated by East European Jews, mostly from Poland and Rumania. It was a virtual "Tower of Babel." One could hear dozens of languages spoken, a lot of "broken" Hebrew, and the most peculiar linguistic combinations. I cannot forget an instance in which the mother of a girl I had befriended attempted to convey to us that she was going to the market to buy a chicken. What she said was, "*Ani holekhet kupit' kukuryku*." The first two words (I'm going) were in proper Hebrew. The third word (to buy) was in Russian (the woman came from Chernovitz in the Soviet Ukraine), but I was particularly amused by her choice of word for "chicken." She opted for "*kukuryku*," the Polish onomatopoeic word denoting the sound made by a rooster (the equivalent of "cock-a-doodle-doo").

Our next-door neighbors were musicians from Hungary. They, too, produced amazing linguistic formulations. Later the man became my first piano teacher. While he spoke to me in Hebrew, I still recall clearly his specific Hungarian intonation.

My parents enrolled my sister and me in the neighborhood school. One picks up languages quickly as a child, so by the beginning of the school year, we could already understand most of what our teachers were saying and in no time could follow their lessons without difficulty. The only class I found challenging was *Tanach*. The language of the Old Testament was a far cry from the conversational Hebrew taught in the summer class.

I quickly made new friends at school. Among my closest friends was Rita, a girl from Iraq; Anat (formerly Ania), who came from Russia via Poland; and another girl from Poland, Zosia, who was given the Hebrew name Tzofiah. A special friend was an Israeli-born girl, Irit Zeisel, who helped me with my Hebrew assignments and whose family "adopted" me as a new immigrant, often including me in various festivities at their home located high on Mount Carmel. As a blond, blue-eyed girl I was favored among my classmates and invited by them to birthday parties and other fun activities.[2]

My friends and I ventured to the beach at Bat Galim to swim in the Mediteranean, went to see movies in the "Tchelet" movie theater, and climbed up the slopes of Mt. Carmel to pick up alpine violets and other flowers. Boys started showing interest in me, and every Friday night, my entire class would participate in hora dancing on the Kiriat Eliezer promenade. In short, I was very happy in Israel. I loved the climate and felt free: the country enveloped me. While in Poland admitting to being Jewish was risky, in Israel I quickly lost my "Jewish complex." People were friendly and reached out to help. My days were filled with true *joie de vivre*. The two and a half years I spent in Israel were the best part of my childhood; I had a sense of belonging which I have never regained in my subsequent nomadic life. Of course, I was too young then to fully understand the nature of Israeli society, its culture and politics, the complexity of Israel's conflict with the Arabs, and the challenges Israel faced given the instability of the Middle East.

My parents were not so blind and adjusted to Israel differently. Both of them found jobs in Haifa. My mother was hired as a clerk in *Misrad Haotsar* (Treasury Department), and Father found employment as a researcher at Bet Erdstein, which later became the University of Haifa. (His Hebrew was very shaky at the time, so I sometimes wonder what his tasks were.) Yet while Mother was content on the whole, Father was not.

Within a year of our arrival in Israel, my parents' intense discussions about returning to Poland began. Mother wanted to stay; Father wanted to leave. My sister and I were not consulted. While we knew what was going on, being children, after all, we managed to ignore the debates and fill our days with fun.

My mother did solicit advice from friends and relatives. Most of them sided with Mother and condemned my father for not being patriotic and for even contemplating "out-migration." Yet that was what my Father was determined to do. He could not tolerate the hot Israeli climate: on at least two occasions, he fainted in the street and was brought home by an ambulance.

---

[2] The preferential treatment of blond girls continued for years, as I learned when my daughter attended third and fourth grade in Jerusalem during my stint there as director of an overseas program for American students in 1982-84.

The political climate of Israel was also not to his liking. Moreover, he was surprised and disappointed to have discovered the essential silence about the Holocaust in Israel, the reluctance to speak about it. Survivors were seen as weaklings and victims, and those who had perished were referred to as "cattle led to slaughter." Even speaking Yiddish was discouraged, as it was viewed as the language of victims. This outlook has changed by now, but it was extremely pervasive in the late 1950s. For all of these reasons Father could not acclimate to Israel. I suspect that being professionally demoted and viewed as a weakling, in contrast to the brave Israelis, must have been unbearable for him.

The debates about staying or leaving continued for months. Some cousins suggested that my mother let her obstinate and foolhardy husband go back to Poland, but that she and the children (meaning me and my sister) should definitely stay in Israel. At one point, Mother decided to follow their advice. It was then that Mother solicited my opinion. The answer I gave her was, "I want to have a Mommy and a Daddy." I still marvel at the diplomatic way I found to avoid taking sides.

Partially because of my response, I suspect, my mother decided not to break up the family, and to return to Poland. Her decision was also prompted by a "turnaround" of some of the friends and relatives who had earlier encouraged her to stay. When Mother had appeared ready to remain in Israel, they were suddenly frightened that a single woman with two children might become a burden on them. So now their advice was, "*Me furt mit dem man,*" which translated from the Yiddish means "one goes with one's husband." We returned to Poland in December of 1959.

Chapter Five

(Temporary) Return to Warsaw

During and after World War II, migrations and the dispersion of Jewish families were extremely commonplace. Polish Jews ended up living on practically all the continents of the world. Over the years, I have read and heard about countless sagas of Jewish survivors. My family's story entailed the previously mentioned migrations within Poland and Ukraine, the return to Poland in 1946, three transplantations in Silesia, and then emigration to Israel in 1957. These were fairly common routes for many survivors. However, our return from Israel to Poland in December of 1959 was a rather unique move back. Very few Jewish families chose to move to Poland in the late 1950s, or were permitted to do so.

The years 1956-1957 were a period of a political "thaw" in Poland, and Jews were allowed to emigrate. Thousands took advantage of that opportunity. My father had succumbed to the "herd instinct," due primarily to pressure from my mother. Despite his grave apprehensions about moving to Israel, we had applied for permission to emigrate. When notified that permission was granted, Father had gone to pick up the passports, yet reluctant to burn bridges with his native land, had insisted that the words "with the right to return" (*z prawem powrotu*) be stamped in his document. He prevailed. These few words inserted in his passport gave him, and by extension our entire family, the legal basis to reclaim Polish citizenship.

* * *

We arrived in Warsaw in December of 1959, in the middle of the coldest winter in anyone's memory. Indeed, the media referred to it as "the winter of the century" (*zima stulecia*). After two and a half years in Israel's warm climate, we were particularly sensitive to the cold. My parents' close friend and fellow survivor, Andrzej Bryl, took us into his two-bedroom apartment. He, his wife, and his two little children all slept in one bedroom, while our family of four settled in the other. Andrzej and his family were exceedingly gracious for the first few days and certainly appreciated the many gifts (mostly articles of clothing) my parents had brought them from Israel, but in no time—quite predictably—hosting a family of four in a small apartment with a tiny kitchen and one bathroom became a burden. Tensions arose. Alas, it took a whole month for us to be able to move out. The shortage of housing in Warsaw was so severe at the time that renting an entire apartment was virtually impossible, but my parents did succeed in finding a room for rent. We moved in with the family of a very talkative seamstress. She hardly ever left the apartment, and the visits of her clients were quite frequent; finding any privacy was virtually impossible.

Despite that, my father revived emotionally in Warsaw. He was tremendously relieved to be able to function in Polish, his native tongue, and delighted to see his native city being rebuilt. In due course, he started teaching in the Teacher's College (*Studium Nauczycielskie*) on Stawki Street and also got involved with TSKŻ, the Social and Cultural Jewish Society, becoming a contributor to its newspaper, *Folks Sztyme*.

Mother coped as best she could. She focused on taking care of me and my sister, and soon started teaching Russian in a high school, but I could sense that she was "grinning and bearing it."

Our living conditions kept improving. About a year after our return to Warsaw, we obtained an apartment of our own in a block on Broniewskiego Street in the Muranów district, and a few years later we moved to an even better apartment in the district of Zolibórz at 8 Braci Załuskich Street in a new development called Sady Zoliborskie.

* * *

From my perspective as a 14-year-old, the contrast between my life in Israel and my life in Poland was initially overwhelming. I felt miserable and missed my Haifa friends. After the space and freedom I had enjoyed in Israel, I found myself confined in more ways than one. Warsaw was an unfamiliar city.

Chapter Five | (Temporary) Return to Warsaw

Being a minority again—that is, being one of three Jews in a class of forty—was a drastic change after Israel. (The other two Jewish girls were twin sisters, Maja and Wanda Rawicz. One of them, Wanda, shared my desk until our high school graduation.) I had to adapt to a different mode of functioning and revert to caution in order not to expose my "otherness." Truth be told, I resented my father for having brought us back to Poland, but seeing how hard it was for my parents to establish themselves in the new city, I kept my feelings mostly to myself. I kept silent, but inwardly I resolved to return to Israel when I was old enough to make independent decisions about my life.

Gradually, however, I adjusted to Warsaw and made new friends. I even came to like the high school I attended, *Liceum* #1 at 15 Felińskiego Street. Most of my teachers were excellent. To this day, I owe a debt of gratitude to Mrs. Pawlowska, my Polish teacher, who instilled in me a love of literature. Mrs. Zapasiewicz, my math teacher and the mother of the distinguished actor Zbigniew Zapasiewicz, is also a teacher I remember fondly. While my history teacher, Mrs. Starzyńska, widow of Stefan Starzynski, the pre-World War II president of Warsaw, had a difficult time maintaining discipline in her classroom, I learned a great deal in her classes as well. Other teachers who linger in my memory were Mrs. Liberowa, who taught Latin, and the chemistry teacher, old Mr. Salvin. The latter almost succeeded in persuading me to undertake the study of chemistry at the university. I would have done so were it not for a random conversation with a professional in that field. She told me about the chemical stench one had to endure in the lab on a daily basis and the deleterious effect of many chemicals on one's health.

Around 1961, special psychological tests (*testy psychotechniczne*) were introduced in Poland, intended to help graduating high school students determine their university major. In the Polish educational system, one had to make that important decision at this critical moment in life. Having selected a specialization, one applied to the appropriate university department and, if accepted, followed the major from the freshman year on. While the results of my test gave me many other options, I applied to the English department of Warsaw University. I was interested in becoming a foreign correspondent and thought knowing English well would be an asset. The School of Journalism comprised a two-year program one could enroll in only after obtaining a university diploma in another field. (I soon gave up the idea of becoming a journalist. The more I was exposed to the foreign press as a student of the English department, the more I realized the degree of censorship in the Polish media.) Primarily, however, I wanted to obtain a degree in English, so that I would have another option—that of teaching English in Israel. I still thought that I might emigrate after obtaining my MA.

One incident that strengthened my resolve to return to Israel occurred when I was 16 or so. A boy, a classmate of mine, began showing interest in me. It was a very innocent "courtship," which began with his surreptitiously leaving unsigned folded pieces of paper containing rose petals on my school desk. Eventually he invited me to go on a bike ride with him. I accepted his invitation, and on a lovely spring Sunday we went for a ride in the Bielany district. A day later, quite accidentally, I learned that he was beaten by his parents for going out with a Jew. My sister's girlfriend happened to be my potential boyfriend's next door neighbor, and she heard his parents' yelling and the boy's screams when he was being punished. While visiting my sister the next day, she gleefully reported to me—I still recall her words—"Ale Paweł dostał wczoraj lanie!" (What a beating Pawel got yesterday!). Then she proceeded to provide the details of what she had overheard.

What saved me from a persistent sense of "otherness" were Jewish summer camps. When I was fifteen, my parents sent me to camp for the first time, to one organized by TSKŻ (The Social & Cultural Jewish Society). It was in Poronin, a little village near Zakopane in the Carpathian Mountains. The following year, I attended another camp on the Baltic coast. At age nineteen, after my sophomore year at the university, I worked at one of the camps, Węgorzyno, as a counselor. I cannot overstate the importance of those camps to me. I made lifelong friendships there, some of which have lasted more than 50 years now. I learned many Yiddish songs, which I remember to this day. The camps provided me with opportunities for fun, for tourist adventures, and for exposure to Jewish culture—secular Jewish culture, to be sure. Above all, the camps were oases of psychic comfort for me. I could be myself and drop caution to the winds, forgetting briefly my fears of saying something that my Catholic classmates might perceive as ignorant or odd.

Although I had eventually acclimated to my life in Poland, a lingering desire to return to Israel remained. Having graduated from high school at 17, I began my studies at the English department of Warsaw University in

Chapter Five | (Temporary) Return to Warsaw

the fall of 1962. The following year, as a beneficiary of my parents' extreme generosity, I went to Israel for the summer. My parents had no foreign currency to pay for flights or for travel on trains abroad, but one could pay in zlotys, the Polish currency, for travel on Polish boats. They made the appropriate arrangements and I embarked on the Polish cargo ship SS Oliwa in the Baltic port of Gdynia.

In addition to the crew, there were only twelve passengers aboard. I shared my cabin with a mother and her little boy. Whatever inconvenience the crying of the child caused me was compensated for by the tourist opportunities the trip provided. Every few days the ship stopped in a different port to load or unload some cargo, and each time for a few days I was free to sightsee and explore. SS Oliwa stopped in Kiel, Germany; Rouen, France; Casablanca, Morocco; Piraeus, Greece; Istanbul, Turkey; and finally Haifa, Israel. Since it was very difficult to obtain permission to travel in those years, and for financial reasons as well going to so many countries would have otherwise been impossible for me, I was thrilled.

Unexpectedly, while I was in Morocco, my knowledge of Hebrew turned out to be an asset. As soon as I disembarked in Casablanca, I met some Jewish employees in the port. I happened to pass a man wearing a chain with a Star of David and said "Shalom" to him. He responded in Hebrew and we started chatting. Soon other port employees emerged and joined in the conversation. As a Jewish girl from Poland, I must have been an exotic visitor for them. The next day was Saturday, so they invited me to a picnic by a swimming pool and came to my ship, my moving hotel, to pick me up. A memorable part of that outing was seeing, a first for me, a poolside competition for the most shapely male legs in Casablanca. Particularly surprising to me about this contest was that, in the interest of fairness I suppose, the men covered their heads and torsos with bags and exposed only their legs. I was also taken on a trip to the capital, Rabat, where I saw not only the royal palace, but actually the king himself as he was coming out of the main gate.

While in Greece, I ventured to Athens and savored the atmosphere of that city. In Turkey, in addition to visiting the tourist sights in Istanbul, I also managed to go to Izmir. After exciting six weeks in Israel, I returned by boat to Italy and by train via Yugoslavia to Poland.

It was, as I have mentioned, very difficult in those years to obtain permission to travel abroad, and legally obtaining foreign currencies to pay for such travel was virtually impossible, but the trip I took in the summer of 1963 instilled strong wanderlust in me. To maximize my potential opportunities to travel, I completed a special course offered by the Student Association to become a guide for foreign student groups visiting Warsaw. I did this for two compelling reasons: guides were given priority in student travel to the countries of the Soviet Bloc, and guiding foreign groups gave me an opportunity to practice my English. While most of the groups I ended up guiding were Scandinavian, students from Great Britain and the United States occasionally came as well, so I was exposed to native speakers of the language. Two British girls I had befriended came back on a private visit and stayed with my family. They, in turn, invited me to England. Thus, in the summer of 1965, I actually visited an English speaking country for the first time. For me, an English major, it was a most important and valuable experience.

Another memorable trip of mine occurred during the university's spring break the following year. Having acquitted myself well in my tasks as a Warsaw student guide, I was selected to go on a short excursion to Moscow and Leningrad. What I recall to this day was the massive inundation with political propaganda. In the student dormitories where we stayed, there was a speaker installed close to the ceiling in every room. There was no switch to turn it off, and patriotic Soviet songs and speeches were being transmitted non-stop. When we got on the buses taking us around the cities, similar transmissions were made, often interfering with our guides' comments. One day—it may have been April 22, Lenin's birthday—I must have heard Lenin's name mentioned at least 50 times.

I realized during that trip that while the propaganda methods in Poland were considerably more subtle, Polish authorities did resort to political propaganda as well. One example was the flood of anti-German films and statements in the Polish media. As a result, antipathy to the Germans, particularly West Germans, was pervasive among my peers. I still recall the sobering effect of an accidental conversation I happened to have with a West German student who was attached to a Scandinavian group I was guiding around Warsaw. Since the rest of the group knew each other and the German student was an outsider, I invited him to sit next to me during our lunch. He opened up to me during that meal and told me what a burden it was to be a German travelling abroad. Wherever he went, he sensed that people were automatically assuming his family had a Nazi background, when, in fact, his parents and other relatives had been imprisoned and in camps because of their opposition to Hitler. I must confess that this conversation evoked my empathy for him and opened my eyes.

And yet the residual effect of the anti-German movies we were saturated with in Poland remained. I realized that when I had the opportunity to go to East Germany on a trip organized especially for Warsaw student guides. It entailed visits to East Berlin, Leipzig, Dresden, and Meissen. I recall my negative reaction to the tone of speech of our German guide, and particularly the way I cringed seeing marching soldiers. The harsh sounds and high, rigid steps of the soldiers disturbed me, reminding me of scenes from propaganda films. I had a similar reaction when, after graduating from Warsaw University in 1967, I started teaching in the College for Foreign Languages, and as a member of a small group of faculty was sent to East Berlin to meet colleagues from our sister institution. The objective was to discuss and compare our teaching methodologies, but we were also taken on a sightseeing tour of the eastern part of the city, which was still divided at the time. I happened to witness a change of guard in front of some monument and the soldier' motions, particularly their goose steps, disturbed me again.

That trip to East Berlin was my last foreign venture as a Polish citizen.

* * *

During my youth in Warsaw, in addition to traveling I very much enjoyed going to the theater. Warsaw had a number of excellent theaters, all of them state-subsidized and most of them producing very good spectacles. Students received special discounts, so I could afford going quite often, and did so. Theaters also fulfilled a special function in those years: many political and social commentaries that would be the basis for political persecution if expressed openly were conveyed through innuendo in various productions of plays. One went to the theater to get those *sub rosa* messages, as well as to be entertained and enlightened.

Another source of pleasure and enlightenment in the years preceding my departure for the United States was my short period of study at the Yiddish Theater of Warsaw. Headed by the famous actress Ida Kamińska and her husband Marian Melman, the theater produced performances in Yiddish. Most of the audiences did not know the language and relied on simultaneous translation into Polish read by Wiktor Melman, Kamińska's son, which one could listen to by resorting to earphones. As a second-year student at the English Department of Warsaw University, I learned that the Yiddish Theater had opened a training program for young actors. Most of the performers affiliated with the theater were getting on in years, and the special program was launched to ensure a new generation of actors. I signed up and joined a small group of trainees. As most of the theater classes were in late afternoons, I managed to reconcile them with my classes at the English department.

While I realized very quickly that I did not have a sufficiently strong ego to be an actress, I received a most valuable education during the year and a half that I participated in the program. Classes were offered by senior actors as well as invited lecturers. I learned a great deal about the history of Jewish and world theater and studied the Yiddish language and classics of Yiddish literature, as well as performance skills and even stage make-up. Additionally, of course, I had the privilege of briefly studying acting with Ida Kamińska, the star of the theater and a charming and very talented woman. We students also had many opportunities to watch the experienced actors perform. Among them were Ruth Kamińska, Ida's daughter, Abraham Samuel Retig, Karol Latowicz, and a younger actor named Henryk Grynberg. Their faces are still vivid in my memory.

* * *

In 1968, notorious events came to pass which resulted in my family's dispersion. I left Poland in August of that year to pursue graduate studies in the United States (which will be discussed in detail in the next chapter), while my parents and sister departed a year later.

Reading Teresa Torańska's book *Jesteśmy: Rozstania '68* recently, I made the discovery—shocking to me—that Jews expelled from Poland after March 1968, whose typical route involved being processed as refugees in Vienna and then waiting in Rome to see which country would accept them, travelled in sealed train cars on the Vienna-Rome section of their trip. According to Wanda Gruber's testimony, included in that book, the former Polish citizens, now holders of the infamous "travel documents" which declared them stateless, were viewed as high-risk passengers, and the trains were sealed so they could not escape.[1] Friends of mine, Anna and Wladyslaw Zajac, who emigrated the same year my parents did, confirmed that on the train they were closely watched and repeatedly counted by the Austrian gendarmerie up to the Austrian border and then by Italian police. My parents had never mentioned this to me, but if that was still the practice when they made the Vienna-Rome trip, I can imagine how humiliating and disturbing the experience of travelling under surveillance must have been for them. The echoes of World War II experiences would have been inescapable.

When I think of my parents' and my sister's arrival in Vienna in June of 1969, I still recall my distress that I could not be there to meet them. I did not have a "green card" (that is, permanent resident status) yet, and was unable to leave the United States. The one consolation I have is that, through sheer serendipity, an Austrian exchange student I knew was returning to Vienna at the end of the semester and agreed to meet my parents at the train station. He handed them my written message and a gift of some $30. That was all I had been able to save out of my meager scholarship. At least my parents received a token of my deep care, love and concern.

---

[1] Teresa Torańska, *Jesteśmy: Rozstania '68* (Świat Książki, Warsaw, 2008), 265.

Chapter Six

1968; or, America! America!*

I was caught up in the 1968 wave of Jewish emigration from Poland. To rely on a well-worn metaphor, that is when my personal "exodus from Egypt" occurred. The decades that followed were my years of "wandering in the desert" (in more respects than one) and searching—as I still am—for the "promised land."

In one of the ironies of fate, unlike most Polish Jewish refugees of the infamous year 1968, I—with literally about $10 to my name—travelled to the United States in style.[1] Having embarked on a luxury boat, the SS *Rotterdam*, in Rouen, France, I spent five days being wined and dined on that vessel, and docked at Pier 51 in New York City on September 8, 1968. Of the 600 passengers on board, only four, including myself, were in their twenties. The others, mostly American retirees, were ladies and gentlemen of leisure, proudly displaying their gold watches, diamonds, and mink stoles. The voyage, which included lavish meals at the captain's table, struck me as rather surreal.

* * *

---

* This chapter was originally written in 2008, on the 40th anniversary of my arrival in the United States. A slightly modified version was published in *Polin: Studies in Polish Jewry* 24 (2012): 401-411.

[1] In 1968, the limit on foreign currency one could officially purchase at the National Bank of Poland and take out of the country was a mere $5. I managed to buy a few extra dollars from friends whose American relatives had a habit of inserting one-dollar bills into their letters. As mail from the West was routinely inspected, not all the money reached the addressees. Fortunately, some did.

Chapter Six | 1968; or, America! America!

The circumstances surrounding my departure from Poland were a mix of curses and blessings. On the one hand, I had left Poland as a persecuted Jew, deprived of Polish citizenship; on the other, I was going to America on a full graduate scholarship, a rare privilege for any Polish citizen in those days.

Having graduated with an MA in English from Warsaw University in 1967, I began teaching at the Warsaw College for Foreign Languages (Studium Języków Obcych), as well as part-time at the Warsaw Polytechnic Institute (Politechnika Warszawska), in the autumn of that year. I hardly ever visited Warsaw University after my graduation. I did, however, venture there on March 8, 1968, International Women's Day. That holiday is observed throughout Poland to this day, with women receiving flowers not only from their boyfriends and husbands, but also from their bosses, supervisors, and co-workers. Feeling a debt of gratitude to the librarians of the English department collection, who had valiantly assisted me in locating materials for my master's thesis, I saw March 8 as an appropriate occasion to express once again my deep appreciation. I went to the Warsaw University campus that morning and delivered bouquets of flowers to them.

My mission accomplished, I was briskly approaching the university's main gate when I found myself confronting a line of auxiliary policemen, members of the ORMO.[2] Their arms locked and their sticks prominently displayed, the men advanced steadily, hurling insults at students. A large number of buses could be seen behind them, with more and more police descending from them, all in a clearly bellicose mood. The tension was palpable and the danger of being assaulted imminent. Well familiar with the campus, I quickly ran to a side gate and managed to escape unharmed. A lot of students and other visitors were not so lucky. They were beaten, arrested, and thrown in jail.

I came home deeply shaken: this was my first direct encounter with organized brute force. My sense of shock continued for weeks as the unfolding nightmare hit closer and closer to home. The next day, the names of Jewish students, particularly those which did not sound typically Polish, were published in the newspapers, to create the impression that Jews were stirring up trouble and creating unrest. I was acquainted with some of the students and knew that they were totally innocent.

---

[2] Voluntary Reserve of the Civil Militia (*Ochotnicza Rezerwa Milicji Obywatelskiej*).

In the months to come, hundreds of students were expelled from universities, and some were arrested. Purges of Jews from various positions were occurring with increasing frequency. My father, who taught modern history at Warsaw's Teachers' College (Studium Nauczycielskie) on Stawki Street, was fired from his job. His transgression, as he was told explicitly, was teaching his students about the Warsaw Ghetto Uprising and taking them to the monument to the heroes of that historical event, a monument located just around the corner from the college. He was asked to apologize for his "offense" (in the spirit of the self-criticism (*samokrytyka*) practiced quite often in the Soviet Union and its satellites), but he refused. That period was harrowing for my father, whose leftist leanings surfaced even before the Second World War and who believed in the promises of communism, particularly those of ethnic and religious tolerance. He felt a deep sense of ideological bankruptcy, and his distress was painful to watch.

My mother, who until March 1968 had been awarded various prizes as an exemplary educator, resigned from her job as a high-school teacher of Russian when her students welcomed her one morning by pounding on their desks and chanting, '*My się żydowskiego uczyć nie będziemy!*," (We will not study the Jewish language!).

While I retained my jobs, I too experienced a number of very unsettling moments. I recall in particular walking with my mother on Marszałkowska Street, one of Warsaw's major thoroughfares, and noticing the animosity, the glares of hostility, directed at her. As we left a store that sold Chinese arts and crafts, I even heard a derogatory comment. Olive-skinned and dark-haired, Mother was the classical Semitic type, and the stares and words of the passers-by were unmistakably hateful. Instantly, I drew closer to my mother and took her by the arm. It was an instinctive reaction to protect her. Given her Holocaust experiences, I felt that she certainly did not deserve to be yet again subjected to such expressions of antisemitism.

Another moment I recall with profound sadness was a scene I witnessed right in my neighborhood on my way home from work. Two boys, no more than 7 or 8 years old, were fighting. I recognized one of them as a former pupil, whom I had taught English in an extracurricular afternoon class at the neighborhood elementary school. What I found so disturbing was the nature of the abuse I overheard the boys hurling at each other. The words, which are lodged in my memory to this day, were "*Ty żydzie!*" (You Jew!). I realized then that those children, who could hardly have known who or

Chapter Six | 1968; or, America! America!

what a Jew was, were already growing up with this horrible prejudice and were using the term "Jew" as an insult. I was so upset then that I could not even bring myself to intervene and stop the fighting, which I certainly would have done under normal circumstances.

The direct impact of the events of March 1968 on me and my family was emotionally devastating. Indeed, I must confess that I left Poland with a profound sense of insult and humiliation. Abuse directed toward Jews was rampant in the months prior to my departure. The state-controlled Polish media were totally unrestrained, all of Poland's economic woes were blamed on individuals with Jewish-sounding names, and *Trybuna Ludu*, the Communist Party newspaper, printed various "expert opinions" that were cruelly demeaning to the Jews. One writer, for instance, alleged that the Jews stemmed from a colony of lepers in Egypt.[3] Statements echoing *The Protocols of the Elders of Zion* abounded. On the state-sponsored TV news one could see crowds of factory workers yelling insults and carrying banners with antisemitic inscriptions like "*Mośki do Izraela!*" (Kikes go to Israel), or more indirect ones, like "*Precz z syjonizmem!*" (Down with Zionism). Some, like "*Syjoniści do Syjamu!*" (Zionists to Siam!), bordered on inanity. The terms "Zionist" and "cosmopolitan" were routinely used as synonyms for "Jew," and carried most derogatory connotations.

The Communist Party Secretary, Władysław Gomułka, who became the Polish Ramses, not only condoned the abuse but had no qualms about making insulting comments of his own, for example by referring to Jews as sympathizers to Israel and denouncing them as the "fifth column." Not surprisingly, many Jews who had been loyal Polish citizens left the country.

* * *

The opportunity to study in the United States was a most unexpected development in my life. Warsaw University had an established tradition of inviting Fulbright Scholars to teach in its English department. In the

---

[3] On February 25, 2013, reading Adam Kirsch's review of David Nirenberg's book *Anti-Judaism: The Western Tradition*, I learned that there exist sources dating to ancient Egypt which make similar prejudiced assertions (e.g., one from an Egyptian priest named Manetho, who claimed that the Jews of the Exodus were "lepers and other unclean people"). http//www.tabletmag.com/jewish-arts-and-culture/books/123971/a-world-without-jews

academic year 1966/7, Professor Sy Kahn from the University of the Pacific in Stockton, California, was the Fulbright Scholar in residence. I signed up for his American literature classes, and he also became my thesis advisor. Shortly after I submitted my master's thesis on "The Concept of a Hero in Bernard Malamud's Writings," he invited me to his office. I assumed that he had suggestions for revisions. Instead, he praised my thesis and, looking me straight in the eye, asked, "How would you like to continue your studies in the United States?" His university did not have a graduate program, he promptly clarified, but he knew of several excellent ones. The school he recommended in particular was the State University of New York at Binghamton, which offered graduate scholarships to foreign students. It was too late to apply for the academic year 1967/8, Professor Kahn told me, but he encouraged me to do so for the following year and promised his strong support. I remember that beautiful day in May distinctly, and clearly recall rushing home to share the good news with my family, and literally jumping for joy.

I followed Professor Kahn's advice and applied to the English Department at SUNY Binghamton. In early 1968, I received notification of my admission to the graduate program, and my challenge became to obtain a passport. To get one, I first had to secure a leave of absence from the College for Foreign Languages, my primary employer. Several times I spent hours waiting in the offices of the Kuratorium (the Education Department) without ever being allowed to see any of the officials. Before attending the office in person, I had sent in multiple written applications, which had also been ignored. Without a formal statement certifying that I was granted leave, the passport office refused to issue me a passport and I could not leave the country. While I may have been confronting the standard bureaucratic treatment, I perceived the lack of response and the constant evasions of the various officials as forms of chicanery, and that view was supported by the fact that all over Poland there were other blatant instances of discrimination and abundant evidence that the antisemitic campaign was in full swing. I eventually reached the conclusion that the only way for me to take advantage of the incredibly rare opportunity of continuing my studies in the United States was to renounce my Polish citizenship and leave Poland as a Jewish refugee, pretending to head for Israel.

In June 1967, following the Six-Day War, the Polish government had cut off all diplomatic relations with Israel. The Dutch embassy in Warsaw

Chapter Six | 1968; or, America! America!

took over, and handled applications for Israeli visas, which then became the basis for obtaining the infamous "Travel Document" (*dokument podróży*) one could use as an exit passport. The Document was a one-way permit which stated explicitly that the bearer was not a Polish citizen. To obtain this document one also had to present a paid-for ticket to Israel. Since my destination was Binghamton, New York, and not Israel, I resorted to a subterfuge. I appealed to my relatives in France to send me train tickets from Warsaw to Paris and from Paris to Marseille, as well as a ticket for a passage by sea from Marseille to Haifa, with the plan of exchanging them once I arrived to Paris. To my immense gratitude, they obliged, and these were the tickets that I presented.

My itinerary was rather unusual, as most other Polish Jews opted for a more direct route to Israel, mostly travelling by train to one of the Italian ports and then by boat to Haifa. Not surprisingly, I was treated with much suspicion. After weeks of explanations and much pleading, however, I was allowed to use my French tickets and was issued the Travel Document. By the time I finally held it in my hands, I was a nervous wreck.

To add insult to injury, I was also made to repay a huge sum of money for the allegedly "free" education I had been offered by the socialist state. 30,000 zlotys—a horrendously high amount, given that 2,000 zlotys was the average monthly salary—was the fee imposed by the Polish authorities on emigrating university graduates in the humanities. The fee was even higher for holders of degrees in the hard sciences. After pleas and negotiations, the sum I was ultimately made to pay was reduced to 20,000 zlotys, as I had already taught for a year. Needless to say, I had no funds to meet even this lowered demand. I owe my parents an eternal debt of gratitude for the incredible sacrifice they made by offering me all of their savings to pay that extortive fee.

These were but some of my pre-departure vicissitudes. Another one emerged in the process of obtaining a US visa. When I first went to the US embassy in Warsaw to seek clarification regarding visa application procedures (very aware that plain-clothes policemen were watching me as I entered the building), the US consul received me warmly. He seemed most sympathetic. Appalled by Poland's deployment of the same criteria as those behind the Nuremberg Laws in Nazi Germany, as he told me, he was resolved to grant me a "green card," that is, a permanent resident visa. America, he claimed, needed people like me, young and educated.

Yet when a few months later I showed up in his office with the Travel Document in hand, he apologetically admitted his reluctance to instigate an "international diplomatic incident," given the deteriorating political situation in Poland, and declared that he could not give me an immigrant visa after all. Instead he gave me a tourist visa. Rather than stamping it into the Travel Document, however, he issued it on a small piece of paper (3 by 5 inches) and instructed me to hide it well, assuring me that I would be able to obtain permanent residence once I landed in the United States. Thus I was leaving Poland as a stateless person, not knowing a soul in all of America, and with merely the hope, but no certainty, of becoming a US resident.

In late August of 1968, my family, the fiancé I had by this time, and a number of my friends came to see me off at the Gdańsk railway station (*Dworzec Gdański*) in Warsaw. While engaged in tearful personal farewells, I could not help noticing the several trains which zoomed by, carrying Polish soldiers to Prague. The "fraternal army" of the People's Republic of Poland was assisting the Soviet Union in quelling the Czech rebellion. That shameful collusion also contributed to my sense of disdain as I left for America.

Before I reached my destination, however, I first went to France, where I was entertained for a few days by my father's cousins, whose father had emigrated to France in the 1930s. They promptly returned my Paris-Marseille and Marseille-Haifa tickets to the travel agency, replacing them with a ticket for the SS *Rotterdam*, which turned out to be cheaper than the air fare to New York City. My elaborate scheme to get to the United States had worked!

Although the SS *Rotterdam* was a luxury liner, my trip to New York was not entirely a "love boat" adventure. I was travelling with a heavy heart, fearful that I might not see my parents, my sister, and my fiancé for years, if ever again. I was also experiencing a state of anxiety about the unknown. Shortly after the ship's departure from Rouen, moreover, I found out that one of my two suitcases had been lost. It contained, among other items, my Olivetti typewriter, a priceless possession for me in those days. In addition to these difficulties, there was yet another source of disquiet and stress: on the second day of the trip, one of the stewards started making very unwelcome advances towards me. I even found him opening my cabin with a master key! While I threatened to notify the captain about his outrageous

Chapter Six | 1968; or, America! America!

conduct, I had no way of knowing if he would heed my threats. (Mercifully, he did!)

My only contact in New York City was Anna Tenzer, the sister of a Warsaw acquaintance of mine, Szmul Tenenblat, the editor of the Yiddish newspaper *Folks-Sztyme*. I did not dare write to Anna from Poland, afraid to give away my "conspiratorial" plan of going not to Israel but to the United States. It was only after obtaining my ticket for the SS *Rotterdam* that I sent her a postcard from Paris. I had never met Anna, as she had emigrated to the United States some ten years earlier, but Szmul assured me that she was magnanimous and would welcome me in New York. There was no way of knowing, of course, if she would, nor was I even certain that my postcard, which contained information about the place and time of my arrival, would reach her in time.

When the SS *Rotterdam* docked in the New York City harbor, I looked around, scanning the huge crowd on the ground for anyone who could possibly be Anna. I had no idea what she looked like. Fortunately for me, the postcard I had mailed from Paris just a week earlier had reached her. Anna showed up with her husband, Moniek Tenzer, and let me know she was there with a piercing scream "Are you from Poland?" Never before was such a dissonant sound so pleasing to my ears. I waved at her and established eye contact. My sense of relief was enormous: here was someone on this foreign shore who could assist me and advise me.

Little did I know that I would subject the kind couple to a very long wait. Of the 600 passengers on board, I was the last to disembark. The immigration officers in New York had never seen a Travel Document before. They were equally surprised to see a visa on such a small piece of paper. I could not blame them for eyeing me with great suspicion. After questioning me and making phone calls to their supervisors and to SUNY Binghamton, however, they ultimately allowed me to leave.

Anna and Moniek Tenzer assisted me in more ways than one. They drove me to their house in Brooklyn, fed me, hosted me for two days, and lent me money for the bus fare to Binghamton. The fare was $13 in those days, and my entire dollar budget of $10 had been diminished by $5 on the train from Warsaw, when at the East German border I was forced to pay a $5 fee for a transit visa, with the threat that I would otherwise be removed from the train. This was a totally unexpected expense, and an insult added to injury, since Polish citizens could cross the border without any visas. As

I learned later, Moniek, whose father had died a few days prior to my arrival in New York, decided to forgo his filial obligation to go to the synagogue and say prayers and waited patiently for me to disembark. I am most grateful to the Tenzers for their generosity and kindness to this day. I must admit, however, that when on my second day in America they tried to "fix me up" with Moniek's younger brother Icio, who had a drinking problem, I suspected them of an ulterior motive. This matchmaking attempt was not the only surprise that awaited me.

If truth be told, my exposure to Brooklyn was a real culture shock. I found myself surrounded by people speaking "broken" English, with working-class mannerisms I was not used to and, most surprising of all, they did not look at all like the actors I had seen in Hollywood movies. Their appearance was a far cry from what I had seen on the screen. "Where are all the handsome and tall Americans?," I wondered. The same question crossed my mind at Binghamton, where the vast majority of students were rather short New York City Jews. I soon realized that although I had read a great deal of American literature and thought I knew something about the United States, I had come to a totally foreign land.

Among my other shocking discoveries were the unlimited amounts of food students were allowed to load onto their trays in the university cafeterias and the incredible waste of food I witnessed all around me. It bothered me terribly to see students engage in mock fights and toss rolls at each other, or throw mountains of uneaten food into the garbage. I also had to adjust my monetary scale. Given the exchange rate back in 1968, the average monthly salary in Poland was $20. Thus, spending a quarter on a can of coke or a bag of pretzels dispensed in the vending machines in my dormitory struck me as most extravagant.

The dress code on campus was yet another culture shock. Both students and faculty dressed casually, in stark contrast to the fashion requirements in Warsaw, particularly on my daily route on Krakowskie Przedmieście, where one walked to see and be seen. In Binghamton, even when I thought I was rather shockingly underdressed, I was repeatedly asked by fellow students, "What did you dress up for?"

Although fashion etiquette definitely was not the primary reason for my disenchantment, I must confess that after the initial few days of discovery, when the novelty of Binghamton wore off and the colors of the autumn foliage diminished, I missed Warsaw terribly. I felt trapped on

Chapter Six | 1968; or, America! America!

the campus and in the provincial town where it was located, and missed the big-city atmosphere. Sights of Warsaw, particularly of the Nowy Świat street, repeatedly appeared in my dreams for several years after I left it.

As soon as I settled in my dormitory at Binghamton and enrolled in my courses, I focused on getting my family out of Poland. My mission was twofold: first, to persuade my parents and sister to leave Poland, and second, to find ways to bring them to the US I plunged myself into a letter-writing campaign to HIAS (the Hebrew Immigrant Aid Society) and other agencies. I wrote to congressmen and senators (and indeed still have Senator Jacob Javits' letter of reply). My five-hour bus trips to New York City to intercede directly were quite frequent. (It wasn't until a year later that I bought a car from a departing French student for a sum total of $50. This bargain, a beaten-up Corvair, almost cost me my life and could have burned down an entire building. I had parked in front of my dormitory, and as I was pulling out one day I saw flames leaping high from the engine at the back of my car. Fortunately, Petr Bjaček, a Czech graduate student, saved the day. He had the presence of mind to yell "Get out!" and located a fire extinguisher, which he used, effectively saving my life and perhaps the lives of others.)

My parents did not know any English. Still, I was hoping to find jobs for them. I also searched for study opportunities for my sister, who had completed three semesters of a course in veterinary medicine in Warsaw. Alas, I soon found out that easing my parents' entry into the United States was a pipe dream. There was little I could do for them. Likewise, I could be of little help to my sister. Practically no funding was available for foreign undergraduates at that time, and there were totally different requirements for veterinary medicine majors in the United States than in Poland. To begin with, in Poland veterinary medicine was a course of study one began as a freshman; in the United States it was a graduate program. In addition, a lot more general education at the undergraduate level was required in the United States than in the programs of study at Polish universities.

Luckily, after leaving Poland in 1969 and following the standard route of Polish Jewish refugees—that is, being processed in Vienna and then waiting for several months in Rome—my parents managed to settle in Paris and in due course obtained French citizenship. My sister stayed in Italy, enrolling at the University of Perugia, from which she later graduated with a degree in veterinary medicine, and where she met her husband. She became an Italian citizen. During her initial period in Italy, I helped her to the best of my ability by sending her small sums out of my assistantship, which amounted to $2,500 in 1968 and increased to $2,750 in the following years. I had better luck bringing my fiancé to the United States. He obtained a graduate fellowship at the philosophy department at SUNY Binghamton and joined me fifteen months after my departure from Poland. We got married a few weeks after his arrival in the United States.

All along, while trying to help my family and my future husband, I also had to do well in my studies. At least a B average was required each year in order to have the teaching assistantship renewed for the following year. Not only was I competing with American graduate students, and thus at an obvious linguistic disadvantage, but as a TA (teaching assistant) in a literature and composition class, I, the foreigner, had to teach American undergraduate students how to write in their native language. At first, that made me feel very awkward and tense. When I got the first batch of my students' papers, however, I relaxed considerably. I recognized there was a lot I could teach them even though English was not my native tongue. Still, my *English Pronouncing Dictionary* was in constant use. I was meticulous about checking the pronunciation of unfamiliar words, and spent hours preparing for my classes.

As the first student at SUNY-Binghamton from behind the "Iron Curtain," I was viewed as an "exotic animal" of sorts, that is, with curiosity and caution. While curiosity got me invited to some professors' homes, the university decided to play it safe, and my MA from Warsaw University was not recognized. I had to embark on a second MA program before I could proceed towards my Ph.D. To capitalize on my knowledge of foreign languages and literatures, I decided to get my second master's in comparative literature. By 1973 I had managed to get my Ph.D. and to my surprise was offered a teaching position in the comparative literature department there for the next academic year.

What I remember most distinctly from my first year at SUNY Binghamton is that my agenda was drastically different from that of other students. In the autumn of 1968 there were protests against the Vietnam War on campus. The SDS (Students for Democratic Society) was quite active and vocal, advocating civil rights and other noble causes, and especially "making love, not war." After President Nixon's election, the mood on

Chapter Six | 1968; or, America! America! 97

campus was somber. Many students, as well as professors, were visibly upset, if not heartbroken, about the outcome of the election, and many intensified their political activities. Yet their concerns, I must confess, were on the margins of my interest. I had other issues on my mind. I was trying hard to strike roots in America and help my parents, sister, and fiancé start a new life as well. These basic existential issues preoccupied me to such a degree that I had no psychic energy left for anything else.

My preoccupations were also in sharp contrast to my roommate's. She was a very attractive Austrian girl from Graz who came to the United States for a year of fun. Funded by her well-to-do father, who, as she had told me, called her his "piggy bank," she viewed her classes as secondary to parties and good times. Indeed, young men were routinely invited to our room. After a few weeks, one of them emerged as the leader of the pack. I would often come back from the library to find my room bolted from within. The next year, I arranged to be an RA (resident assistant), which meant additional responsibilities, but also a room of my own.

By then I had also obtained immigrant status. A few weeks after my arrival at Binghamton, William Derbyshire, a professor of Russian who took me under his wing, had accompanied me to the American Civic Association in downtown Binghamton to file my visa application. The clerk informed us about the immigration law at the time, which stated that as I had no relatives in the United States, and was not married to a US citizen, my only option was to apply under the Fifth Preference category, that is, as one having a rare competence few or no Americans could boast. While I instantly thought my chances of obtaining an immigrant visa were nil, Professor Derbyshire, demonstrating typical American positive thinking, was undeterred. In our casual chit-chat on the way downtown I had regaled him with my experiences teaching ancient Greek drama in the literature and composition class. To my total surprise, he used that information and, without batting an eye, presented me to the American Civic Association clerk as a great expert in ancient Greek drama. I remained speechless. Miraculously, his argument worked. Shortly thereafter, I became a permanent resident, which allowed me to travel to France and see my parents.

Only now, as a parent of grown children, do I fully understand how painful my decision to go to the United States must have been for my parents, who had lost their entire families during the Second World War. There was no way of knowing if they would ever see me again. It did not help that in 1968, when I was leaving Warsaw, the assassinations of John F. Kennedy and Martin Luther King, Jr., were fresh in their memories and made them see the United States as a wild and dangerous country. My mother, as both she and my sister told me much later, cried non-stop for two weeks after my departure. Fortunately, we were able to reunite, albeit for a short time, after only a two-year hiatus. For a family as close as we were, that was a long time. Likewise, the geographical diffusion that followed our departures from Poland required painful emotional adjustments for all of us.

A lingering sense of injustice regarding the 1968 events in Poland stayed with me for quite some time after my arrival in the United States. I must confess, though, that I felt generally misunderstood in America as well, even by American Jews. I recall distinctly a conversation with another graduate student at a wine and cheese party at Binghamton. Asked why I had left Poland, I poured my heart out, telling her about the antisemitic campaign and the various humiliations experienced by Polish Jews. Having listened intently (or pretending to do so) for quite some time, she asked me, "All right, but other than for financial gains, why did you come to the US?" I was dumbfounded by that question, and jumped to the conclusion that it was pointless to share my thoughts with Americans because our frames of reference were so drastically different. Financial gain was the last thing on my mind when I struggled to get out of Poland.

That sense of not being understood has stayed with me to this day, and my closest friends, not surprisingly, are people who share my background. Among them are Ala and Włodek Konar, who came to the United States in 1969 and that summer generously let me stay with them in their apartment in Brooklyn. My graduate scholarship payments ended in May 1969. While my assistantship had been renewed (for five years, as it turned out), if I wanted to survive until September 1969, the beginning of the next academic year, I desperately needed a job. None were available in Binghamton. After all, thousands of students were competing for the few local opportunities. My solution was to go to New York City, where I succeeded in finding a "brain-dead" office job on Broadway near 34th Street. My one-and-a-half hour commute from Brooklyn by subway was a new and not very pleasant experience, but walks around Manhattan on my lunch breaks were fun. So were my good times with the Konars. It was in their company that in the summer of 1969 I saw man's historic first walk on the moon.

Chapter Six | 1968; or, America! America!

* * *

Today, years after my departure from Poland, I also recognize the many positive outcomes of what back in 1968 I perceived as my misfortune. I am aware of the cognitive privileges of exile; I am appreciative of the many opportunities America has given me and my children; I realize that the world has opened up to me in ways it definitely would not have, had I remained in Poland. Above all, I know that my years in America have cured me of the inferiority complex I felt in Poland as a Jew. I've learned not to apologize for who I am.

To return to the biblical metaphor, my "exodus from Egypt" was a blessing in disguise. Although what America offered me, the "manna from heaven," figuratively speaking, was unfamiliar nourishment, at least at first, and often accepted reluctantly and with a longing for the familiar foods of yore, in retrospect I recognize and appreciate the value of that "manna." My decades in the desert (emotionally and spiritually) were a period of major transitions and self-discovery. Gradually, my regrets and nostalgia for the past have vanished.

I have learned to forgive and forget. Eventually, I even had no qualms about becoming a cultural ambassador, promoting Polish literature in the United States as a translator, scholar, and teacher. I also ventured back to Poland for several academic conferences and visits. I considered my stint as a Fulbright Research Scholar in Kraków and Warsaw in the academic year 2001/2 as the triumphant return of an abused citizen.

There are days when I think I may well have reached "the promised land." On other days, it still seems to be a mirage, a Fata Morgana.

Chapter Seven
Dreams

During my high school and university years in Poland, the centralized system of public education there adhered closely to the Communist party line. I was taught to be dismissive of religion, of any forms of mysticism, and even of psychoanalysis. My own father's atheistic outlook and condemnation of both religion and superstitions as the residual beliefs of the unenlightened and uneducated (he often resorted to the Yiddish phrase "*bubeh mayses*," that is, old wives' tales) reinforced in me a firm adherence to rationality and critical thinking. Indeed, one of the Latin maxims my father imparted to me, "*Audiatur et altera pars*" (Listen also to the other side), has been indelibly etched in my mind. For years I have favored empirical evidence and searched for scientific foundations, solid methodologies, testable hypotheses, and verifiable evidence to support any claim. Thus brainwashed, I considered my friends' assorted superstitions to be very suspect folk wisdom and I found the interpretation of dreams an idle and silly pursuit of the simple-minded.

However, my mother, a very sensible and educated woman, was not as judgmental or dismissive of "irrationality." She certainly believed in dreams and did not shy away from interpreting them. Some of the prophetic dreams she had during the war were of utmost significance to her. One of them concerned the appearance of her deceased sister Chaja (pronounced Haya).

* * *

Seven years older than my mother, Chaja was born in Brześć. She graduated from a private Jewish high school and was both an excellent student and an exceptional beauty. Olive-skinned and dark-haired, she was nominated once for Miss Brześć, a local beauty pageant.

In the early 1930s, following the untimely death of her first love, a rabbinical school student, who had succumbed to typhus, Chaja got engaged to Malkil Pinczuk (who had the same last name as my mother's family, but was of no relation to them). Their wedding took place at the Hotel Ritz in Bialystok. A paternal aunt, Pelta Zylberblat, who had studied medicine in St. Petersburg and then married and moved to Bialystok, made all the arrangements for the special venue, and more than a hundred people attended the wedding.

Following their honeymoon, the newlyweds settled in Brześć and soon had a son whom they named Szalom (pronounced Shalom). Chaja hoped that her next child would be a daughter, whom she planned to name Bracha (which means blessing), so that combined the children's names would add up to a phrase of welcome in Hebrew—"peace and blessing" (*Shalom u-Vraha*).

Malkil Pinczuk owned, jointly with his mother, Cypa Pomeraniec, and his brother, a big fabric store. In the 1937 Brest Taxpayers roster he was listed as a merchant residing at 14 Kosciuszki Street, and his mother as residing at 24 Dąbrowskiego Street.[1] They were fairly well-to-do, despite the pogroms in Brześć which often resulted in the store being raided. My mother remembered the scenes of robbery and devastation she witnessed, with bales of fabric being appropriated, or deliberately soiled by the Polish men. They tossed fabric into mud, or tied it around and between trees. Still, Malkil was able to afford a beautiful house on a tree-lined street. His was among the first houses in town with indoor plumbing. Friends and acquaintances would come to admire the modern conveniences: the bathroom with a flushing toilet, a built-in bathtub, and a shower, all of which were novelties at the time.

When the Soviet Army occupied Brześć, they requisitioned the house for one of their officers. Chaja, her husband, and their six-year-old son were forced to move into one little room. The Soviets declared Malkil a capitalist and intended to send him and his family to Siberia, but the new tenant, a Soviet officer from Leningrad who happened to be Jewish, took pity on

---

[1] http://www.brest-belarus.org/rd/tax1937/Brest1937/taxpayers_P.i.html.

the young family and interceded with the Soviet authorities on their behalf. As a result, they were evicted, but instead of being sent to Siberia were given the option of choosing their own destination. Chaja and her husband decided to go to the town of Kovel, where her paternal uncle Israel (Srula), the owner of the local sawmill, was in position to take them in.

When the Germans occupied Kovel, however, the whole family found itself in the ghetto. Chaja's husband built an underground bunker for them to hide in, and soon they had to retreat to that bunker. Little Szalomek, as he was affectionately called by the family, behaved well for a while, but then, starving and thirsty, started crying. Whether Chaja was forced to leave the hiding place or left voluntarily in consideration for the safety of others, or followed her maternal instinct and ventured out in search of sustenance for her child, I do not know. All I know is that she and the boy came out of hiding.

As soon as they found themselves in the street, a German soldier noticed them. Pointing a gun at Chaja, he led them to a nearby town square. He humiliated Chaja in public by calling her insulting names, made her let loose her beautiful long hair, and forced her to take her coat off. Thus exposed to abuse and cold, Chaja and Szalomek were made to wait until a hefty crowd gathered around them. The German soldier then inflicted on Chaja the worst pain a mother can experience: he shot Szalomek in front of her, first positioning him so that she could see the execution without any obstructions. Minutes later the soldier shot Chaja as well.

A woman who had witnessed the whole scene conveyed the devastating news to Malkil. Shortly thereafter, having bribed a Polish policeman, Malkil escaped from the Kovel ghetto and made it to Brześć, where he imparted the terrible news to his in-laws. Thus my mother and her parents learned of Chaja and Szalomek's murder. Alas, Malkil did not survive the war either. He, his in-laws, and his brother-in-law all perished. [2]

---

[2] The only member of Malkil's family who survived was a brother, who had left Poland before the war to study medicine in Italy. He later immigrated to the United States, where I met him and his wife in the autumn of 1968. They lived in Queens, New York, at the time. He changed his name to Maurice Pine and had two children, a daughter and a son. I have not kept in touch with them.

Chapter Seven | Dreams

* * *

Some time after Malkil's report, when my mother and her family were hiding in a bunker in the Brześć ghetto, she had her first "prophetic" dream. She dreamed that Chaja had come to her, extended her hand, and said to her in Yiddish, "*Kim mit mir!*" (Come with me). In the dream, my mother was overjoyed to see her beautiful older sister and was about to follow her when her deceased grandfather appeared and grabbed Chaja forcefully by her shoulder, saying, "No! She will not go with you." When my mother woke up, she gave a detailed account of her dream to my grandmother Rifka. The latter declared, "This means that you will survive the war." My mother firmly believed that it was her grandfather's intercession that had saved her life.

Mother often made comments about fate, destiny, and the unpredictable and unintended consequences of the choices one makes. She wondered if Chaja and her family might not have survived, had they been deported to Siberia.

* * *

Mother had another dream when she and her family were in the Brześć ghetto that she told me about. As the Germans were constantly making demands for Jewish property, often under the threat of death, her family decided to hide some of their most precious possessions. Her father and brother, both being very handy, managed to hide the family's expensive clothing and furs under the kitchen floor, and some of the jewelry under a few stove tiles which were removed and then replaced. A neighbor, who must have been spying, denounced them and had no qualms telling her brother about it. The whole family was terribly anxious about the impending visit of the German police. That night, my mother had a dream that the Germans came, but found nothing and left empty-handed. And that was indeed what happened.

I have previously mentioned, in the chapter titled "Bialystok," another dream Mother considered important. In it, her mother Rifka told her, "My dear Masha, I'll buy you a nice red dress." The next day, under the most unexpected circumstances, Mother was shown a lovely red dress that fit her perfectly. She bought it and, given the rare opportunities to obtain such nice garments during the war, considered it her murdered mother's gift to her.

When I was in my thirties, Mother told me of another dream in which my grandmother Rifka had appeared. This one, too, I touched upon it in the chapter "Białystok." Although she had always been a very dutiful daughter, and remembered clearly her mother's frequent admonitions to remain Jewish, and particularly her mother's words in the Brześć ghetto "*Maszele, zolst gedenkn, di zolst hasene hubn mit a yid*" (My dear Masha, remember, you should marry a Jew), my mother was nonetheless reluctant to tie the knot with my father. The night before my parents were married, grandmother Rifka appeared in my mother's dream and advised her not to marry my future father. Mother was astonished by this admonition. She confronted her mother, saying, "But he is Jewish. You've always told me to marry a Jew!" Rifka's reply was, "Yes, but with this one you will never be happy." During the occasional less-than-happy moments in my parents' relationship, Mother would refer to this dream and state wistfully that she should have listened to my grandmother.

Mother certainly ascribed meanings and significance to dreams. I recall her telling me that dreams about a baby portend bad news, and that when excrement appears in a dream that is a good omen. I must confess that while I listened, I viewed such notions with intellectual distance. There was even a certain unexpressed condescension in my views of Mother's dream interpretations, and other evidence of her "irrationality." She would cite, for instance, the German saying which translates as "A spider seen in the morning brings bad luck, but seen in the evening brings good luck on the third day" (*Spinne am Morgen bringt Kummer und Sorgen; Spinne am Nacht bringt Glueck am Drittag.*) and seemed to believe it, and she would tell me that itching in the palm of the left hand means "money is on its way," but that itching of the right hand signified a forthcoming and unexpected meeting of a friend.

Mother would also resort to fake spitting (with the onomatopoeic rendition of it in Polish as *tfu, tfu, tfu*) whenever she heard some bad news. She would routinely augment it with the Yiddish phrase *nisht ba keinem gedaht* (may it never happen to anyone). When I was still living at home, practically each time I was about to go out she would ask me to put a pinch of salt in my pocket, or my purse, to avoid the evil eye (*a git oyg*). The tiny packets of salt which became commonplace in fast food restaurants, or in airline meals, were routinely saved by my mother and given to me for that very purpose. On occasions when Mother thought I was particularly well dressed or seemed very happy, she would look at me admiringly and utter the Yiddish phrase, also meant to ward off the evil eye, "*Zaltz in di oygn, pfefer in nuz*" (Salt into the eyes, pepper into the nose). The mere utterance of these words was intended to incapacitate any potential sender of the evil eye.

Indeed, I learned a great deal about Jewish folk beliefs from my mother. One custom that struck me as particularly bizarre was smacking a girl gently in the face (*a patch in punem*) when she got her first period, which I learned about when my daughter reached that watershed moment of transition to womanhood—I don't recall whether I received the same treatment at that time in my life.

I heard many of my mother's tales reflecting Jewish folk wisdom over the years, but given my rational bend of mind, I accepted them with a grain of salt (pun intended). These were snippets of the Jewish tradition she passed on to me. Writing about these superstitions may seem odd in a book about the Holocaust, but they are an integral part of a bygone era; they are reflections of Mother's mentality formed by her childhood in Brześć and my way of recapturing the family's past in a culture that has disappeared and that I was never able to know first-hand.

* * *

My dismissive attitude concerning dream interpretation changed drastically after an unusual dream of my own in Buffalo, New York, in the early 1990s. It was a very vivid and visual dream. In it, four Hebrew letters appeared to me against a bluish-grey background. I remember waking up with a sense of wonder, because I hardly ever dreamed, or at least hardly ever remembered my dreams when I awoke. I also wondered about the meaning of the four letters I remembered so distinctly. Not sure if I retained the order of the two middle letters correctly, I started putting them together in alternate sequences in my mind, and concluded that the only sequence in which the letters made sense was the one in which they spelled the name Meir. The image of the four Hebrew letters lingered in my mind. I wondered for days what it meant, and who was sending me a message—in Hebrew letters no less!—and why. I could not come up with an answer. I did not know a single Meir personally, so the dream was very much an unanswered riddle.

While visiting my parents in Paris a few months later, I casually mentioned my bizarre dream over lunch. My father's reaction was instantaneous: "What do you mean you don't know any Meir? My name is Meir!" This was the very first time I heard my father's real name. He had used the name Teofil in Poland, and when he was writing for the Yiddish press he used the first name Tovyeh. I had assumed all along that Tovyeh was his real Yiddish name, all the more so as it appears as my patronymic in the Ukrainian birth certificate I was issued in Dubno. I had no idea, though I had known my father for close to 50 years, that Meir was his given name! The fact that I learned it due to a mysterious dream shook the foundations of my rationality, and I started viewing much more sympathetically the many people, among them famous and intelligent people, who were open to mysticism, spiritualism, and interpretation of dreams. It was because of that dream that I was propelled to engage in further inquiries and speculations. The dream was essential in my making the leap away from strict rationality toward greater openness.

I recalled that Homer accorded divine origin to some dreams and Plato declared dreams as divine manifestations to the soul in sleep. Much later, in the nineteenth century, the "*crème de la crème*" among the French intellectuals believed in apparitions and dreams and gathered regularly at the Paris salon of Madame Blavatsky, the pioneer of esoterics. In his book *Premonitory Dreams and Divination of the Future*, the French astronomer and author Camille Fammarion (1842-1925) wrote, "I do not hesitate to affirm at the outset that the occurrence of dreams foretelling future events with accuracy must be accepted as certain."[3] Perhaps my mother was right.

More recently, top notch scientists acknowledged the limitations of strictly scientific methods in fathoming reality. As Albert Einstein (1879-1955) proclaimed in his often quoted statement:

> Try and penetrate with our limited means the secrets of nature and you will find that, behind all the discernible concatenations, there remains something subtle, intangible and inexplicable. Veneration for this force beyond anything that we can comprehend is my religion.

---

[3] Camille Fammarion, *Premonitory Dreams and Divination of the Future* (Whitefish, MT: Kessinger Publishing, 2010), 6.

In his book titled *Life Beyond Death* (2012), which was on the *New York Times* best seller list for months, the highly trained neurosurgeon Dr. Eben Alexander, MD, revealed that he had found the hyper-reality of the spiritual realm. He advocates a deeper probing into our consciousness and a symbiosis of science and spirituality.

Gradually, I have grown less skeptical about my mother's prophetic dreams and have come to believe that dreams are inherent to our consciousness and in some ways still very mysterious to me are bound up with the faculties of reasoning. Indeed, our minds are wondrous instruments and our bodies are mysterious. While I would have been embarrassed to acknowledge it even a few years ago, lately, when good things have happened to me (and I have been fortunate in that many have…) I cannot dismiss the fleeting thought that perhaps somehow I owe them to my mother's intercession.

I also chose to attach a symbolic significance to the fact that my second granddaughter, Nessa, was born on the 66th anniversary of the liquidation of the Brześć ghetto; that my sister's granddaughter, Rebecca, was born on our mother's birthday; and that my third granddaughter, Levia, was born on on the anniversary of my mother's death.

The lines Shakespeare's Hamlet addresses to his loyal friend Horatio—"There are more things in heaven and earth, Horatio, than are dreamt of in your philosophy"[4]—lately ring more and more true to me.

---

[4] "Hamlet" (Act I, scene 5).

Chapter Eight
Dwelling in a Name

"I dwell in Possibility," the poet Emily Dickinson proclaimed.[1] This lofty line makes me think of the various other mental spaces we inhabit. One of the foremost is that of our own names. While a name is given to each of us at birth, usually by our parents, and we have nothing to do with the choice, we tend to "dwell" in our names for the rest of our lives. Some do rebel and change their names, or assume nicknames, but most people endure the names given to them, even if they don't like them. There are, of course, a lucky few who are happy with the names chosen for them, and most people accept their names tacitly, never bothering to contemplate the issue.

I, however, have had a problem with my given name—and its origin is quite complex. My name was decided upon by both my parents, who, having lost their entire families, felt a moral obligation to commemorate their loved ones. One way they envisioned doing this was by selecting a name for me, their first-born, which would preserve the memory of not one, but several of their lost relatives. My parents composed a list of the people dearest to them and attempted to create an original name for me out of the initials of their perished relatives' names.

Of their various rather awkward creations, the one they almost settled on was the name "Gromol," which included the initials of their parents: G for my paternal grandmother Gela; R for my maternal grandmother Rifka; M for my paternal grandfather Mojsze; and L for my maternal grandfather Lejb. Fortunately, my mother averted the disaster by using the powerful argument that such a first name would rhyme with my last

---

[1] http://writing.upenn.edu/~afilreis/88/ed-possibility.html

name, and Gromol Grol would inevitably make me the object of classmates' ridicule at school. Ultimately, my parents settled on the name Regina, which contained my two grandmothers' initials, and that is the name that appears in my birth certificate.

Not only was my name weighted with the memory of the two murdered grandmothers I was never privileged to know, and pretentious to boot (*regina* is Latin for queen), but the name Regina was also terribly old-fashioned in the Poland of my childhood. I never met another child by that name, and it wasn't until I was 50, and abroad, that I finally encountered a namesake. Frankly, I was not surprised at the rare occurrence of the name in predominantly Catholic Poland. The liturgy in the churches was in Latin, and the word regina was reserved primarily for religious hymns extolling St. Mary as "*Regina celli*," that is, "the Heavenly Queen."

Acutely aware of the odd name I was saddled with (and the fact that I was a queen with no dominion!), I opted for nicknames beginning in my early childhood. Even my parents abandoned my given name. After calling me Reginka (the diminutive form of Regina) for the first four or five years of my life, they too, in addition to unrelated terms of endearment, used assorted substitutes (Renia, Reneczka, Renusia, et al.). "Reniuchna" [pronounced Renyuhnah], a tender diminutive form, was favored by my father. Later, during my university years, Rena was the version most commonly used by my friends. (I also discovered, as a student at the English Department of Warsaw University, that in England "Queen," or "Queenie," was a name commonly bestowed on cows.)

In Israel, where my parents and I moved in 1957, I was given yet another name. The school officials in Haifa wanted to impose on me the old-fashioned name Malka, the Hebrew equivalent of "queen." I rebelled and refused to exchange one old-fashioned name for another, however, and succeeded in negotiating a change from Malka to the upbeat Hebrew name Rina, which means "a joyous song," a name closer in its sound to my Polish nicknames—both those I already had and the one I adopted in university. For two and a half years Rina was my name.

Upon my arrival in the US in 1968, I resolved to accept my original name, Regina. Alas, its pronunciation is different in English. The hard "g" in the Polish pronunciation of Regina becomes "dzh" in English. This I have learned to accept. However, to this day I do not tolerate the second accepted English version where the letter "i" is pronounced as the diphthong "ay."

(Its rhyming with "vagina," I believe, is explanation enough.) Truth be told, I have never felt "at home" in my name, but I have resigned myself to it.

Then, unexpectedly, my calm was undermined—and not only with reference to my first name, but my last name as well. Very recently, in January 2011, I visited Rio de Janeiro and met, for the first time, a branch of my father's family—descendants of Calkie (pronounced Tsalkeh) Nudel, my paternal grandmother's brother.

Calkie had emigrated to Brazil in the 1930s and settled in Sao Paulo, and later moved his family to Rio de Janeiro. In 2003 his grandson, Andre Nudel Albagli, had established contact with me via email, having found me on the internet after a strenuous search. Andre had found my daughter's college email address first, but by that time she had graduated and no longer used it. When he found contact information for me, he met with no greater success: I, too, had changed my email address. Ultimately he located my sister's address in Italy, and through her we finally connected.

Since our initial contact, I had been in touch with Andre via email and occasionally by phone, but I had not seen him face to face. While over the years he has shared with me some news of his grandmother (Calkie's widow, Shana Sura Brajterman; deceased by now), his parents (Calkie's only daughter Ruth and her husband Shlomo Albagli), and his wife Claudia Luz, he had never mentioned his brother Henrique, nor the brother's two sons, Rafael Camel Albagli and Michel Camel Albagli. Our first reunion in Rio, thus, was both emotional and full of surprises. (It should be mentioned that this reunion took place in the only Polish restaurant in Rio, where gefilte fish as well as genuinely Polish dishes were on the menu!)

Andre brought along his family photo album to show me. It contained several photographs my father had sent his Uncle Calkie right after the war. These photographs, mailed in 1946, shortly after my parents had repatriated from Ukraine to Poland, included a baby picture of me, sitting naked and holding a teddy bear, as well as a beautiful picture of my mother and a few pictures of my father. Andre offered to scan the pictures and send them to me. I, in turn, committed myself to translating the inscriptions on the back of the photographs, which were written in both Polish and Yiddish, languages Andre does not know.

True to his word, Andre scanned both sides of the pictures and emailed them to me. When several days after my return to the United States I got around to translating the inscriptions, written in my father's hand,

Chapter Eight | Dwelling in a Name

I was astounded by my discoveries. In Rio de Janeiro I had glanced at the pictures, but my attention had been distracted by concurrent conversations with several of the relatives. Now that I was examining the inscriptions closely, I was quite startled: on the back of my baby picture, Father had written in Yiddish "this is my daughter (he used the affectionate diminutive form *tekhterl*) Rifkeleh." "Rifkeleh" is the diminutive and affectionate form of Rifka (Rebecca)! I never knew my parents had called me that, not even in private. Although my mother mentioned on numerous occasions that I resembled my grandmother Rifka, a well-liked woman whose nickname was Bobbele (a name I passed on to my daughter in her middle name, Bobbie), I had no clue that I had ever been my maternal grandmother's namesake. I surmise that the transition from Rifkeleh to Reginka occurred upon my parents' return to Poland. While I was a blond, blue-eyed baby, and my "Aryan" looks protected me to some extent, my parents were mindful of the pervasive and persisting animosity toward Jews and were probably fearful of stigmatizing me by using a distinctly Jewish name in public, and so used my legal name and variations on it.

Even more startling was my discovery that perhaps Grol was not my father's real last name. On the back of one of the photographs of himself, Father had written a warm dedication to his uncle Calkie and signed it, putting after his last name Grol the name Lopatis (or Lopates, the writing was not clear) in parentheses.

Throughout my childhood and adulthood I knew my father as Teofil Grol. Shortly after my parents moved to France in 1969, my father started publishing in French language magazines and used the French spelling of his first name (Theophile), whereas in the Yiddish press he continued to use the first name Tovyeh, the name listed on my birth certificate. Father's disclosure that his real first name was Meir had, as I mentioned in the chapter "Dreams," occurred when I was in my forties. Subsequently, I have also discovered in the Yad Vashem archives that his maternal grandfather's name was Meir, so for my grandmother Gela to name her first-born son after her father would not have been unusual. Yet the revelation that Father's last name might not have been Grol did not occur till January 2011, when I had just turned 66, and my father had been deceased for 12 years!

The discovery that Grol may not be my "ancestral" name had a strange impact on me. It unsettled me. In the past, I had taken it for granted Grol was truly my family name. While at the Ellis Island museum, I had checked out the name Grol and discovered that it was a fairly common Dutch name. A friend who had visited some Jewish cemeteries in Belgium reported to me that she had seen the name Grol on some of the graves. From these sources I had speculated that perhaps my father's family had Sephardic origins and at some point migrated from Spain via Holland to Poland.

I had never run into anyone by the name of Grol in Poland, but in 2006, during a Polish Festival in Buffalo, New York, I visited the Polish genealogical research booth and found out that 70 individuals with that last name were identified in Poland, mostly in the eastern provinces. In a country of close to 40 million people, that's a rather low incidence. I ruled out the idea that they could be relatives because I knew my parents had looked everywhere after the war to check if any family members had survived.

Yet I did recall that my father had asked me to look up someone whose last name was Grol when I taught in Israel in the years 1982-84. I attempted to do so and discovered that there were two brothers by that name, but neither was still living. However, I did establish contact with the widow of one of the brothers, Sarah Grol, a professor of Egyptology at Jerusalem University, who was kind enough to meet me and introduce me to her daughter, but, alas, could provide me with no information about her husband's family. So could Grol be my father's real name?

On the other hand, Father had told me several times about one of his escapes during the war, which he wrote up years later and published in France under the title "How Homer Saved My Life." The incident he described entailed his being stopped by a German soldier who, having closely examined his fake papers and his physiognomy, confronted him: "*Du bist doch ein Jude!*" (You are a Jew!). Although Father had blond hair and blue eyes, his long nose made him fit the antsemitic Jewish stereotype. Father managed to evade being sent back to the ghetto, and most likely to his death, by claiming that he was Greek. When the Nazi challenged my father to say something in Greek, Father recited a fragment of the *Iliad* he had learned by heart while in high school. Even though the passage was in ancient, not modern, Greek, the Nazi was persuaded and let Father go. Certainly, under those circumstances, the name Lopatis, which sounds much more Greek, would have served his alibi better than Grol.

Chapter Eight | Dwelling in a Name

In a pre-World War II registry of midwives, I discovered a Gela Lopates. The name matches that of my paternal grandmother, and I know that this was her profession.

Did my grandfather Mojsze change the last name because as a Bund activist (with the monicker "Moyshe der Shvartser") he was in hot water or on the lam for political reasons? Or did my father, given his political involvements, have a similar motivation to change his name before the war? He told me about his leftist leanings, and his reminiscences about his incarceration as a political prisoner in Bereza Kartuska before the war were included in the volume *Bereziacy*.[2]

I also knew that Father had family in Brześć and that is why he went there after escaping from the Warsaw and Kovel ghettoes. I searched the Yad Vashem archive for people with the name Grol in Brześć and found none, but I did find a picture of a Chaim Lopatis, and his face showed some resemblance to my father. Was Chaim Lopatis, perhaps, my great grandfather?

In short, having found out that my father's last name might have been Lopatis, or Lopates, I was befuddled. I gradually realized that I was unlikely to ever find answers to all of my questions. With so much archival material in Warsaw destroyed during the war, and no one left to ask questions or dispel my doubts, I may never obtain any definitive answers. There is no community to confirm my heritage.

* * *

For several months, each time I would write or type my last name, I had a momentary feeling of alienation, a sense of estrangement from it. I felt somehow "fake," like someone no longer attached to the generational chain linked by the same name.

Then, on October 11, 2011, I had a revelation of yet another kind. I was looking at a piece of paper with my name, Regina, written on it. For some reason (perhaps because I had read some text in Hebrew earlier in the day), I read it backwards. I separated the two syllables, and suddenly two Hebrew words rang in my ears: "*ani*" and "*ger*." The meaning of the words shocked me. The two words mean "I am (*ani*) a foreigner (*ger*)." The words

---

2   Książka i Wiedza, Warszawa, 1965.

epitomized to me my essence as a human being, for throughout my life, wherever I have lived, I have always felt like a foreigner, an outsider.

When I shared my epiphany with a childhood friend of mine, Anat Grebler, a friend deeply steeped in the Kabbalah, she encouraged me to undertake a research project on my name in Hebrew numerology. I have not yet followed her suggestion, but who knows, perhaps one day I will. The significance of numerology, of Gematria, and of letters in general in Judaism has not escaped me.[3]

In fact, one of the first songs my Mother taught me, "*Oyfn pripetchik*," a song about Jewish children learning the alphabet, contains the following words, uttered by a rabbi, "*Und az ir vet kinder elter vern/ vet ir aleyn farshteyn/ vifl in di oysyes lign trern und vifl geveyn*" (And when you children will grow older, you yourselves will understand how many tears and how much pain is contained in these letters). I was launched into life believing in the special significance and importance of letters.

My numerology challenge, should I ever decide to undertake it, would be substantial. Even deciding which version of my name to explore would be daunting!

As has become apparent to me, the answer to the question "What's in a name?" is not so simple.

* * *

The uneasy feeling I had after discovering that Grol may not be my father's real name made me realize how much more disturbing the discovery of their Jewish origin must be for the many people in Poland who find out as adults, decades after World War II, not only that they are Jewish, but often that their parents are not their biological parents. Such discoveries of Jewish origin were not uncommon in other countries as well.

John Kerry, the current United States secretary of state, found out in 2003 (courtesy of a *Boston Globe* journalist) that he had a Jewish grandfather and relatives who had perished in the Holocaust. Likewise, late in her life,

---

[3] In the preface to their book *Jews and Words* (New Haven: Yale University Press, 2012), the co-authors, Amos Oz and his daughter Fania Oz-Salzberger, write, "Jewish continuity was always paved with words." They elaborate this point convincingly in their book. I fully subscribe to this argument: it is primarily in written words that the Jewish tradition has been conveyed.

Chapter Eight | Dwelling in a Name

Madeleine Albright (born in Prague, Czechoslovakia, in 1937), a former US secretary of state and the first woman to hold the position, made a similar discovery about her family. Many more cases of such late revelations and disclosures have occurred.

 The changing of names and the assumption of names that sound less Jewish during and after the war and the only partial sharing of facts about family history by survivors, were common ploys, and I am not alone in my queries and uncertainties. That is another aspect of the lingering legacy of the Holocaust.

Chapter Nine

My Father: The Mystery Man

"To the dead we owe only the truth."

—Voltaire

I am embarking on the writing of this chapter on January 7, 2013. Today would have been my father's 98th birthday. Born in Warsaw, Poland, in 1915, he passed away in Perugia, Italy, on July 1, 1999. I have known him all my life, yet to some extent he remains a mystery man to me.

While Father shared with me some stories of his childhood and youth, and also accounts of his wartime trials and tribulations, there were many lacunae in my knowledge of his past. This chapter is an attempt to put together as many details as I can unearth to preserve the wealth of his lived experience.

While he adored me from the moment I was born, and that was confirmed not only by my mother but also in the accounts and reminiscences of friends who knew him in the late 1940s, for much of my childhood Father, like most men of his generation, was preoccupied primarily with his professional obligations. His involvement in political activities was also intense. Building a better social system seemed more important to him than taking care of his child.

Yet I do have memories of his affection, as well as his various acts of love and devotion. One such act was his standing in long lines every December in the 1950s and 1960s to purchase and triumphantly bring home four oranges, which were rarities at that time. In the post-war period, Poland was rebuilding and focusing on industrialization, so the limited foreign currency it had was not spent on consumer goods or such luxuries

Chapter Nine | My Father: The Mystery Man

as exotic fruit. Thus, oranges were imported only once a year for Christmas, and there was a limit on how many one could buy. I also recall Father's other heroically-obtained provisions. However, the sphere of domesticity was of secondary importance to Father then as it had been during our stay in Israel between the spring of 1957 and December of 1959. As a child I resented this very much.

I also took exception to my father's habit of complimenting and praising me in hyperbolic terms before his friends. He showed a great deal of pride in my accomplishments and bragged about them, which made me feel embarrassed. I thought his praise excessive and therefore never believed it was justified or deserved. One day I confronted him, asking "Why do you make so much fuss over my grades or prizes and keep heaping praise on me?" My father responded instantly. He said that I was living proof of his triumph over the Nazis. They had belittled and degraded Jews, and had thought they would wipe them out, and my existence as well as each one of my achievements was flying in the face of their atrocious plans.

(I must confess that my father's words crossed my mind when my children were born—I had a fleeting sense of similar defiance. The sentiment returned with a vengeance when my first granddaughter was born. I thought to myself, Wow! Here comes the *third* post-Holocaust generation!)

While Father shared with me snippets of information about his past, primarily telling me that his entire family had perished in the Holocaust, I do not recall any lengthy talks with him about his relatives and his wartime experiences until the 1960s. Later, however, I became more inquisitive and he answered my questions more fully.

The crucial facts Father shared with me were that his mother's family stemmed from Warsaw and that his father came from Brześć; that he had a younger brother Marek; that his mother Gela (née Nudel) was a midwife who had studied in St. Petersburg; and that his father Mojżesz (the Polish version of Moses) was a carpenter and a Bund activist known by the nickname "Moyshe der Shvartser."

My paternal grandfather went to Palestine for a visit (I have a vague notion that he was avoiding arrest for political reasons), fell ill there, and upon his return to Poland was diagnosed with stomach cancer. Bedridden and in pain for many months, he died before the war, and both during his protracted illness and after his death the family was afflicted by poverty.

Evicted from the apartment they were renting, they had to move in with my father's maternal grandmother Sura Nudel (née Feterman, b.1872) on Gęsia Street.

Also a midwife, Sura was my father's favorite relative. Not only did she repeatedly bail her children and grandchildren out of their troubles, but she was also affectionate and wise. My father told me various stories about his beloved grandmother's kindness and generosity. The solicitude he showed for most of his life toward elderly women may well have stemmed from that special relationship.

My father loved reading. In his childhood, his favorite author was Karl May, and he adored the German author's stories about the fictional Native American hero Winnetou. Father's other hobby was chess, which he learned to play as a child and continued to play until an advanced age, usually beating his opponents.

Father attended a private Warsaw high school, Gimazium Finkla, on a full scholarship, and received excellent education there. He studied the classics, Latin, Greek, and French.

To underscore the impoverished conditions of his youth, Father told me several times that when he received his *matura*, i.e., his high school graduation diploma, he returned to his grandmother's apartment and was looking for a safe place to put it, but could not find one. The apartment was so small, and packed with so many people, that storing his priceless diploma turned out to be a serious challenge.

As a bright student, Father was admitted to Warsaw University under the Jewish quota (*numerus clausus*), and he recalled with much fondness his professor of philosophy, Tadeusz Kotarbinski.

While I don't know when exactly my father joined the Communist youth movement, I do know that like many young Jews of his generation he was seduced by the leftist ideology. The name Teofil Grol appears in the roster of KZMP (Communist Union of Polish Youth) members for the years 1918-1938, a list compiled by Professor Gabriele Simoncini, which I found online.[1]

Father spoke with great warmth about my grandmother Gela, underscoring her excellent reputation as a midwife. She was also a devoted mother. Not only did she bring him packages of food when he was a po-

---

[1] http://jozefdarski.pl/1128-communist-party-poland

litical prisoner in Bereza Kartuska, even though the family had little to spare, but somehow she succeeded in borrowing enough money to bail him out. In that context and in others he described her as a very loving parent.

World War II shook the foundations of my father's life. He was in the ghettoes of Warsaw, Kovel, Brześć, and Wysokie Litewskie, miraculously escaping from each one. His entire immediate family perished in the Warsaw ghetto. Despite his strenuous efforts to learn about the circumstances of their deaths, he never obtained any concrete evidence. I am sure he must have wondered, as I do to this day, if they starved, died of typhus, or were taken from the Warsaw ghetto to Treblinka in overcrowded cattle cars....

While my father told me occasionally about pre-WWII Warsaw, where he was born and lived until the outbreak of the war, most of my information came from literature, such as I.B. Singer's works, documentary films I located about Nalewki and other nearby Warsaw streets, or the manuscript of the unpublished book *Rachela* I was kindly allowed to read by its author, Ilona Gruda. Another more recent source was the Polish National Digital Archive (http://www.audiovis.nac.gov.pl), where I located many pictures of the Jewish quarter. As Father was not fortunate enough to salvage any photographs of his family, I examined closely the faces in those archival images.

A photo of a 1930 demonstration against the Polish government's edict prohibiting Jews to travel to Palestine (sign.1-P-2346-2) drew my particular attention. There were many young people in the crowd. I looked strenuously, wondering if my father, who would have been 15 years old then, might have participated, but saw no one who looked like him. Looking at another picture of a crowd at the Warsaw railway station (sign.1-P-2350) taken in 1933 and labeled "Jews departing for Palestine," I wondered if my grandfather was one of the men in the crowd.

A few years ago, I located my parents' testimonies in the archives of the Jewish Historical Institute in Warsaw. Their depositions were made in the town of Bytom shortly after the war and recorded by Ida Glikszteijn on behalf of the Jewish Historical Commission in Katowice. While in her two-part deposition, dating from 1946, my mother included significant information, such as names of Judenrat members in Brześć and the name of the mayor (Rhode), when it came to her personal history her testimony essentially included only facts she had shared with me directly and which

I have conveyed in other chapters.[2] My father's testimony, dated May 5, 1947, by contrast, contained some details which were new to me.

The heading of his deposition reads: "Towia Groll [sic] born Jan.7, 1915, in Warsaw, son of Mojżesz and Gela Nudel. Teacher before the war, currently board member of the Jewish Committee in Bytom. Residing in Bytom at 18 Mickiewicza Street."[3]

My father's deposition, made in Polish, is rendered below in my translation:

> It was on June 10, 1942, during an *Aktion*, that I escaped from the Kovel ghetto. On the road I met a group of Jews from Prużany who were running cattle and had a certificate permitting them to return to their place of residence once they delivered the cattle. I joined them and thus, semi-legally, made it to Brześć. I decided to obtain Aryan papers and for the time being stayed in the Brześć ghetto. I established contact with former political activists. They had communication with the partisans in Kobryń. Very soon, however, they were denounced and many of them were arrested. I tried to establish new contacts, but the conditions in the Brześć ghetto were very disadvantageous because the Jewish police eagerly cooperated with the Germans. There were constant denunciations to the Gestapo. Despite that, we did have a resistance group and we even liquidated a policeman who had denounced one of the partisans. I found it hard to obtain decent Aryan papers. Although I would frequently leave the ghetto, it always involved grave danger. And so the liquidation *Aktion* surprised me in the Brześć ghetto. The entire night, when the ghetto was being surrounded, I looked for a way to escape, but it was only early in the morning that I managed to jump over a fence and made it to a house on the border of the Aryan quarter and the ghetto. Upon exiting from its gate, I happened upon a German patrol and presented my Aryan document to them. It did not help. They grabbed me. The Germans stood all around the ghetto positioned in a long line, each a few steps away from the next.

---

[2] My mother's testimony is contained in ZIH file #2151 (testimony re: her Brześć experiences dated October 25, 1946) and file #2157 (testimony re: Wysokie Litewsk, dated November 5, 1946). Both depositions were recorded in handwriting by Ida Gliksztejn and stamped *Wojewódzka Zydowska Komisja Historyczna*, Katowice (Regional Jewish Historical Comission, Katowice).

[3] My father's ZIH file is #2614, also recorded by Ida Gliksztejn in Bytom. N.B., My last name is spelled Grol (with one L).

Chapter Nine | My Father: The Mystery Man

They were not supposed to leave their posts, so each passed me on to the next. It was only the last one who started leading me to the gathering place of all the Jews caught outside the ghetto. Dawn was breaking, and it was getting light. I understood that he was leading me to my death.

The Gestapo man was short and appeared to me to be rather slack. I turned to him and told him, "Let me go." He replied: "*Los, los, schmutziger Jude.*" [Get going, get going, you dirty Jew!] I slapped his face, then kicked him in the stomach, his gun fell out of his hand, and I ran away. I ran blindly, jumping over some fences. When I came to my senses, I found myself on Unii Lubelskiej Street. Treading through forests, I reached Wysokie Litewskie, where the ghetto still existed. It was already the second half of October 1942. In Wysokie there was a closed ghetto with 3,000 Jews. The youth was very militant and well organized, ready to get into the woods at any moment. I was thinking all the time of making some arrangements for myself outside the ghetto, but it was not so easy. For the time being, I stayed with some strangers, very decent people, and had a job as a construction worker. The German who employed me issued a registration slip to me with the name "Teofil Grol, a Pole." That piece of paper later saved my life.

On November 2, 1942, the slaughter of the Jews in the ghetto began. Again I jumped over a fence, and a whole bunch of other Jews followed me. Suddenly, we were confronting Germans with flashlights, as it was very early in the morning and still dark. All the other Jews ran back, but I kept walking toward the Germans. I showed them my document and they believed me that I was a Pole. They even yelled to the men at the subsequent posts, "*Durchlessen, das ist Pole*" [Let him through, he is a Pole]. I knew a woman, a teacher from Vilno, who had been living in Wysokie on Aryan papers for some time. I went to her because I knew that she had contacts with the partisans. She wrote out the directions for me, through villages and forests, and forewarned me about the German patrols. But truth be told, I encountered no Germans on the way because they were afraid to venture into the woods. However, the head of each village [*wójt*] had the order to send patrols and deliver suspicious individuals to the Germans. I happened upon such a patrol of two Belorussians, who immediately recognized me as a Jew and started dragging me to come along. I tried to free myself from their grip. I struggled, but I felt I was gone. I screamed that I was a Pole, but they said I would have to explain everything at the police station. And suddenly a miracle happened: two men jumped out of the bushes and yelled, "Stop!" They asked me in Russian who I was and why I was being arrested. I told them everything except I did not admit I was Jewish as

I didn't know who I was dealing with. They led us deep into the forest to a group composed of 40 people.

These were Soviet prisoners of war who had escaped from German POW camps. They were mostly Belorussians, but there were two Jews among them. I realized I was saved and then I told them I was Jewish. They called the two Jews to speak Yiddish to me to make sure I was not lying. I received a rifle; we killed the Belorussian patrol, and I stayed with the group. At first this was a division of General Kapusta, and later of Kosta Kalinowski. I spent a whole year with them in the forest. The Germans chased us from place to place. We made forays against Belorussian patrols. At the beginning of 1943 a group of Jews from the Bialystok ghetto joined us, but they couldn't get used to the harsh conditions of our life and after some time they returned to Bialystok.

By the end of 1943 I had good "Aryan" papers and went to Bialystok myself. I worked in a bakery, and my task was to organize an antifascist group. I was also active as a liaison between our group in the forest and the fighters in the city. Every week I delivered food and medications to the woods, and I brought back guns and literature.

The AK [*Armia Krajowa*, Home Army] was quite active in Bialystok: they killed Germans in the streets in bright daylight. Yet the AK people also killed Jews whenever they had a chance. This state of affairs lasted until they got an order from London [where the Polish government in exile was] not to kill Jews and were instructed that whoever killed a Jew would later answer for it. The closer the Soviet army was, the more the AK people tried to establish contact with the partisans. I was the person who represented our partisan group. The AK treated me very well, but we reached no agreement. Shortly thereafter, on July 25, 1944, the Soviet Army occupied Bialystok and I was liberated.

This testimony hardly needs elaboration. I have quoted it extensively to provide Father's own detailed account. It explains my father's deep and lifelong bond with other men who had been partisans during the war. Not surprisingly, in the one and only novel he wrote late in life, a crucial character is a Jewish partisan from Poland whom the narrator of the novel, once a fellow partisan, discovers in Italy 30 years after the war.

The novel was written in Yiddish but translated into French and published in Paris under the title *C'est arrive en Pologne* (It Happened in Poland) (Paris: edition Droit et Liberte, 1984). In it, Father dealt—perhaps in too didactic a manner, given current literary tastes and conventions—

with wartime and post-war antisemitism. He had hopes that a film would be made based on his novel to promote the cause of tolerance. This dream is unfulfilled so far and in a world of growing antisemitism, who knows if such a film will ever be made.

Both the partially autobiographical novel and Father's other writings make it clear that even with his "Aryan" papers he was constantly exposed to the "triple threat" during the war, as Poles, Jews, and "Bolsheviks" were all prey for the Nazis. My father never forgot that. I know that in the early 1960s he testified in a Nazi trial in East Germany.

* * *

In his youth Father resisted traditional Jewish education and rebelled against the Orthodox mentality. I suspect that even my grandfather, given his socialist, i.e., Bund, activism, had found the world of religious orthodoxy too confining. My father yearned for a perspective still broader than my grandfather's. He believed in progress, in the ideals of enlightenment, and while I doubt he ever aimed at total assimilation, his Jewish studies were selective and mostly dedicated to secular issues. Yet he did delve deeper into Jewish topics later in his life. In his *Geshtaltn un Perzenlehkaytn in der Yiddisher un Velt Geshihte* (Figures and Personalities in Jewish and World History, a book published in Yiddish in Paris in 1976) large sections are devoted to Jewish heroes dedicated to the fight for Poland, to Jewish revolutionaries in Czarist Russia, to major figures in the Zionist movement, and to Jewish writers and intellectuals in Poland in the years 1918-1968.

After the war, Father was hired as a speech-writer for various party officials in Katowice. His oratorical skills were also impressive, and had become apparent early in his life. He could really fire up a crowd. I actually heard some of his public speeches and eulogies: both in Poland and in France, Father participated actively in Jewish commemorative events. He delivered lectures and helped organize various conferences and academies.

After his emigration to France, Father was briefly affiliated with the Centre National de Recherche Scientifique (National Center for Scientific Research) in Paris, but then he became a freelance journalist. His writings were published in the Jewish press in Canada, the United States, Argentina, and Poland, and appeared routinely in *Presse Nouvelle* and other French-language Jewish magazines. He spoke beautiful literary Yiddish and was often invited to lecture in various Jewish communities all over the world, in countries such as the United States, Canada, South Africa, and Argentina. Requests for him to eulogize friends and acquaintances in France were also quite frequent. He was particularly active in my Mother's Brisk *Landsmanschaft* in Paris. On the festive occasion of its 70th anniversary, he was awarded a gold medal for his many contributions to that organization.

I could often sense that my Mother was proud of her husband's growing recognition. She was clearly in a celebratory mood when he became a member of the French Writers' Association (Association des Ecrivains de Langue Francaise). Some of his articles and speeches were published posthumously and she was very moved by that as well. When I was clearing out their apartment in Paris after her death, I found at least two dozen books written in Yiddish and published in various countries with inscribed dedications to my father, or to both my parents.

I must admit that I, too, was pleased to discover several volumes of my father's books on my very first visit to the Yiddish Book Center in Amherst, Massachusetts. I happened to go there with a disabled friend some ten years ago. Upon entering the library, we descended down the sloping handicapped lane, and Father's books were on the very first shelf we faced. It was a lovely surprise.

* * *

Father was a loving and devoted husband. I found a handwritten draft of my mother's war stories, edited by him and then copied by hand. He obviously wanted to leave a record, and collaborated with my Mom on the unfinished project. Indeed, my parents were the proverbial "turtle doves" in their old age. I can still see them in my mind's eye as they walk in the Parisian parks, or sit on park benches holding hands.

Chapter Nine | My Father: The Mystery Man

* * *

I have to confess that at various junctures in my life I had ideological and political differences with my father. At times, I even considered him politically naïve. Now, however, I give him more credit than I did in the past.

For years, I resented him for our return from Israel to Poland. Now I realize that he was protective of me, my sister, and our family; that perhaps he was prescient when he took us out of Israel in 1959. Perhaps he foresaw the lingering tensions between the Arabs and the Jews and the coming upheavals in the Middle East. Perhaps I should have respected his take on political realities. How would I feel if I had stayed and my children and grandchildren would now have to run to shelters? If my son had to join the army, be exposed to ongoing conflicts, and be in reserve duty for years? Having lost a classmate in the Six-Day War in 1967, having lost a cousin (Aluś Pinczuk) who was an officer in the Israeli army, and having seen my other cousin's despair when her son committed suicide after his army service (he could not reconcile his moral code with the military orders he had to follow), I know I would be a nervous wreck. I certainly thought so in 2012 during the eight tense days between November 13 and 21, when missiles were falling not only on the Southern part of Israel, but close to Tel Aviv and Jerusalem, and one fell 50 meters away from my cousin's house in Moshav Timmorim. My heart went out to the people in Israel. While I had a tremendous sense of relief that no new outright war broke out and that my distant cousins, the remnants of my family, were temporarily safe again, I also had a feeling of gratitude to my father that he took me out of Israel.

While the Holocaust and the unsettling events of 1968 were a shock to Father, as were subsequent wars, terrorist attacks, and other horrors on a massive scale, they did not totally subvert Father's ideological moorings, or his political and historical optimism. His belief in the potential for a just and better world never totally waned.

* * *

The recently deceased former mayor of New York City, Ed Koch, buried in a non-denominational churchyard in Manhattan (at the corner of 155th Street and Amsterdam Avenue), had these words engraved on his tombstone: "My father is Jewish. My mother is Jewish. I am Jewish." These three short sentences were a direct quote of the final utterance of Daniel Pearl, the *Wall Street Journal* reporter murdered in Pakistan on February 1, 2002. As I read these words, I thought of my father and his sense of identity. I came to the conclusion that, despite his life-long leftist leanings and his belief in the possibility of a double—Polish and Jewish—identity in his youth, he would have no objection to a similar engraving on his tombstone. In fact, he might have welcomed it. (See my chapter titled "On Graves….") While after their emigration from Poland my parents obtained French citizenship, they never felt French, and *Yiddishkeit* became central to my father's life.

* * *

I realize that people are infinitely complex; that we do not even know ourselves, let alone others, or to quote Oscar Wilde, "Only the shallow know themselves." I know that there is much I do not know about my father's family or his background. I do not even know for sure if Tovyah is his given Yiddish name or an assumed one. Nor am I certain about his last name. I am also aware that no amount of detail can fully reflect my Father's personality or identity. And yet my compulsion to leave a record of his life took the upper hand. I would view not doing so as a sin of omission. Hence this chapter dedicated to my parent, whose moral compass I have always respected.

When Father passed away, I had an irresistible impulse to leave some mark of his existence on this side of the Atlantic. Even though he never lived in the United States, and his friends and acquaintances in other countries were not likely to read an obituary notice in an American newspaper, I placed one in the *New York Times*.

Chapter Ten

Mother and Her Family

> If my boundary stops here
> I have daughters to draw new maps of the world
> they will draw the lines of my face
> they will speak my words thinking they invented them
> they will invent me
> I will be planted again and again
> I will wake in the eyes of the children's children
> they will speak my words.
>
> —Ruth Whitman[1]

All my life I have had a very close relationship with my mother. Although she passed away in 2004, the intense emotional connection I feel continues. I still think of her very often, her pictures decorate my home, and her birthdays are days of special commemoration and contemplation. She was born on December 24, 1921. Over the years, when all around me Christmas Eve was celebrated by my Gentile friends, I celebrated her birthday.[2] On July 8, the anniversary of her passing, I ceremoniously light a *Yahrzeit* candle. Memories of her sustain me.

Polish was the language of our communication throughout my life. Nonetheless, my mother's Yiddish words—"*Es, my kind, es ...*" (Eat, my child,

---

[1] This poem located online in *Southern Ramblings from New England*, 3/12/12. http://ramblings.theoldtry.com/2012/03/if-my-boundary-stops-here.html

[2] The date of birth listed in my mother's official documents (Dec.15, 1922) was erroneous. When applying for her ID after the war, my father could not recall the exact date and provided this incorrect one.

eat …) still ring in my ears, as do her Yiddish terms of endearment, which were addressed to me throughout my life: *shepseleh, feygeleh, fisheleh* (my little lamb, bird, fish). Later in life, she even called me "*mayn malach*" (my angel).

Maszeńka, as I used to call my mother (using the affectionate Polish diminutive form of her name Masza), has been my friend and confidant throughout my life. She was also the one who initiated me into Jewish traditions, which I consider a special gift. Growing up in postwar Poland, I had no access to formal Jewish education for most of my childhood. There were no synagogues and no Jewish schools in the tows where we lived. While I learned Hebrew and familiarized myself with some aspects of Jewish culture during the two and a half years we spent in Israel during my childhood, the education I obtained was mostly secular.

Mother came from a traditional family that cherished Jewish traditions and customs. She claimed to descend from the tribe of Levi, and taught me how to separate my fingers to create the priestly Levite gesture (one I can still make). She had no problems defining her identity: she was Jewish to the core. In fact, she often referred to herself as *a Yiddisheh tokhter* (Yiddish term for a "Jewish daughter" or "woman").

Mother was named Masza [pronounced Masha] after her paternal grandfather, Mojsze [Moysheh] (in Hebrew, the two names are spelled identically when the diacritical marks denoting vowels are not indicated, as they often are not). She was proud of her *yikhes*, to use the Yiddish word denoting pedigree. There was also a touch of pride in her maiden name: she told me that it was mentioned by the great Polish Romantic poet Adam Mickiewicz in his play *The Forefather's Eve*. (He mentions "*Pinczuk czarny*," black, or dark, Pinczuk).

Whatever sense of my perished extended family I have acquired, I owe mostly to my mother. She loved telling me about her relatives, and this may have been her way of grounding herself psychologically both in her present and the past.

Mother's grandfather, Mojsze Pinczuk, passed away just months before she was born. A well-to-do merchant, he traded in wood and had the lumber transported on rafts to far-away places, even abroad. He owned several houses, as well as forests in the Ukraine, near Kolki, and he built a four-story mill in the town Wysokie Litewskie.

Peasants from nearby villages, to whom he often gave flour free of charge, called him a saint, and indeed, he was known for his charitable deeds. A big donor and supporter of the Wysokie Litewskie synagogue, as well as its *gabbai*, he was "the synagogue beadle for forty years" and "a sweet man, a town favorite." These words were in the caption I found under a picture of him taken by Alter Kacyzne, the famous photographer who recorded Jewish life in prewar Poland.[3]

A few years before my mother was born, Mojsze Pinczuk purchased additional forests near Lvov for the enormous sum of 1.5 million rubles. His business grew and spread to other towns, and he was able to employ all of his sons and sons-in-law. Then, in 1920, the forests were nationalized by the Polish government. The shock of this financial blow made all his hair turn grey. In 1921, while walking down the street, my great-grandfather suffered a sudden heart attack, collapsed, and died. He was only fifty-four years old.

Mojsze Pinczuk and his wife Chana (after whom my daughter Hanna is named) had ten children, all of whom were formally educated. One daughter, Pelta, studied medicine in St. Petersburg at a time when few women opted for higher education. My great-grandmother Chana lived to be very old and was treated most reverentially by the family. In her old age, my mother recalled vividly, she sat in a specially appointed armchair, always dressed up, and thus arrayed would "grant audiences" to her children and grandchildren.

Respect for elders prevailed in my mother's family. She was told that when her grandfather Mojsze had entered a room, everybody would stand up. There was a tradition of family dinners, and my great-grandfather was always served first. That custom continued in my mother's house as well: her father was always the first to be served a meal.

My maternal grandfather Lejb was Chana's second son. In addition to obtaining rabbinical *smicha* (ordination), he was a gifted linguist endowed with other practical talents. He loved animals, and could ride horses and took excellent care of them. Although he was very bright and athletic, Lejb had no, or very little, business sense. Thus, in his youth, he chose to work as a forest ranger marking trees (*brakarz*) for his father, while his brother

---

[3] The caption appeared in Marek Web, ed., *POYLN: Jewish Life in the Old Country: Alter Kacyzne* (New York: Metropolitan Books, Henry Holt & Company, 1999), 136.

Israel (Srule) managed the business. Later, Lejb was a lumber merchant in Brześć. Largely because of his generosity toward his poor customers, he did not do well. History repeated itself when he started another business, a petition-writing office. Although he was well qualified to run it—after all, he was an educated man who knew several languages (Hebrew, Yiddish, German, Ukrainian, Belorussian, and Polish)—nonetheless, empathetic and generous to a fault, he could not bring himself to charge poor people for writing their petitions. He also tutored rabbinical school students, often neglecting to charge them.

Mother told me with great pride that my grandfather Lejb was highly respected in his synagogue. On Rosh Hashana and Yom Kippur he was routinely honored by being asked to be the *Baal Tkiah* (the one who blows the *shofar* or ram's horn) and *Baal Kriah* (the Torah reader). (Mother would pronounce these honorific terms as Baal Tkiyeh and Baal Kriyeh.) He was also much appreciated by his neighbors as a person who always had the appropriate tool, nail, or screw for any household repairs, and was willing to share and help out.

Lejb's marriage to my grandmother, Rifka Aviron, was an arranged one. Rifka's father, who according to my mother lived to be 105, was an affluent man. He founded the synagogue on Listowskiego Street in Brześć and built it next to his house. The synagogue functioned until the entry of the Soviets to Brześć. His wife, my great-grandmother Sura Aviron, also reached an advanced age. She lived to be 95, which is astounding given her illnesses and many pregnancies. Married off at age 15, she had 14 children, only two of whom survived: her oldest son, who emigrated to Argentina in the 1930s, and my maternal grandmother Rifka, her last child. The other children died of assorted illnesses. Around the same time that Sura gave birth to Rifka, she was blessed with a granddaughter, her son's child. Family legend had it that occasionally she breastfed both babies.

My grandmother Rifka gave birth to five children, but two of them died early: one, born after Szlomo, died in infancy; the other, a girl, died at age three, a year or so before my mother was born. By the time Mother was a teenager, Rifka had become quite ill, suffering from asthma and gallstone attacks. My mother became her principal and dedicated caretaker. She helped with cooking, baking, and other household chores. During breaks at school, she would run to the market to buy fresh fish for her mother and hurry to deliver it home. Then back to school she ran.

Chapter Ten | Mother and Her Family

Rifka turned out to be a very dedicated wife and mother. She always tried to focus on her husband's positive attributes and never complained about his meager income. She rented rooms to *yeshiva buchers* (rabbinical school students) and even cooked for them, thus securing the funds for her own children's education.

Rifka's older brother's daughter married a man named Glezer, the founder of the first brewery in Brześć. They owned a beautiful house on Dąbrowskiego Street. The brother's other daughter, Rosa (born on March 23, 1920), studied music in Moscow, became an excellent pianist, and started performing in public at the age of 15. Her husband's last name was Tamarkin. In 1937, at age 17 and already married, Rosa Tamarkina won the second prize in the 3rd International Chopin Piano Competition in Warsaw. Subsequently, she gave concerts to rave reviews and, until her premature death of cancer at the age of 30, taught at the Moscow Conservatory. Her recordings of the works of several classical composers are available to this day.

Mother shared with me these stories and many others. She was especially inclined to tell me about her favorite, beloved sibling, her brother Szlomo, who was eleven years older than she was and practically raised her. When she was a baby, he played with her and took her for walks. Later, he read to her and taught her games. Always protective, he impressed her with his wit and his prowess as an athlete. Szlomo was an avid ping pong player who participated in competitions and taught the sport in the Hapoel club in Brześć. He loved swimming, canoeing, and fishing, and was adept at cleaning and cooking fish, skills he imparted to my mother. Mother adored him. She even told me about the beautiful shape of his legs, which made some of the local girls envious.

When the war broke out, Szlomo was 31 years old and still a bachelor. He had fallen in love with a girl who was then married off to another. He had never recovered from that disappointment, and kept rejecting the many overtures of matchmakers and the generous dowries offered to him. Nonetheless, he had an active social life before the war. Among his close friends was Menachem Begin, who emigrated to Palestine and later became the prime minister of Israel.

When electricity was introduced in Brześć, Szlomo quickly learned to install it, to do repairs when it malfunctioned, and to fix electrical appliances. Many friends and neighbors relied on his help, and he acquired the nickname "*Złota rączka*" (A golden hand). However, Szlomo's primary occupation was as the chief accountant in a large firm. When the Soviets took over Brześć, his bosses drafted a contract transferring the ownership of the firm to Szlomo in case they did not survive the war. The contract was buried in the back yard. Alas, both Szlomo and his employers perished during the war.

I wrote briefly about Mother's older sister Chaja in the chapter titled "Dreams," but I shall add a few details here. Chaja was the pride of the family; my grandmother Rifka adored her. She sewed her impressive outfits, braided her hair beautifully, and allowed Chaja and seven of her girlfriends to meet regularly at her house. Quite often the girls would stay till midnight, singing, telling jokes, and playing games. While they were quite noisy and could be heard in Rifka's bedroom, thus interfering with her rest and sleep, my grandmother never objected.

Chaja's first love was a boy by the name of Krakocki from the little town of Żabinka. Two years older than Chaja, he came to Brześć to attend school. He and Chaja were deeply in love and planned to marry and immigrate to Palestine upon the completion of their studies. After his high school graduation, the young man went to visit his family, and while there contracted typhus and died. Chaja was devastated by this heartbreaking loss. It was some time later that she met Malkil Pinczuk, the younger brother of one of Szlomo's friends, and agreed to marry him.

Although my mother admired Chaja, she felt a bit overshadowed by her, and resented having to wear her hand-me-down clothes. All of this changed when Chaja got married. Seven years older, and now well-to-do, Chaja showered her younger sister with attention. She bought elegant dresses for her and exposed her to various luxuries. Even though there was no tradition of celebrating birthdays in the Pinczuk family, Chaja threw a big party on my mother's sixteenth birthday, with wonderful dishes and lavish gifts. My mother remembered that event with particular gratitude.

Emotionally attached to the landscapes of her childhood, Mother often mentioned the rivers flowing through Brześć, that is, Bug and its tributary Mukhavets (Polish spelling Muchawiec), or the resorts near her home town where she spent some of her vacations. She also told me a great deal about her house on 31 Listowskiego Street, the nearby square, and the friends and relatives who lived in the vicinity. She even drew a map for me, which I happen to have retained despite my many moves.

Chapter Ten | Mother and Her Family

Reproduced below is my mother's attempt at recapturing her neighborhood. She marked on her sketch the names of her relatives, a bakery, a grocery store, a hospital, and a dentist's office.

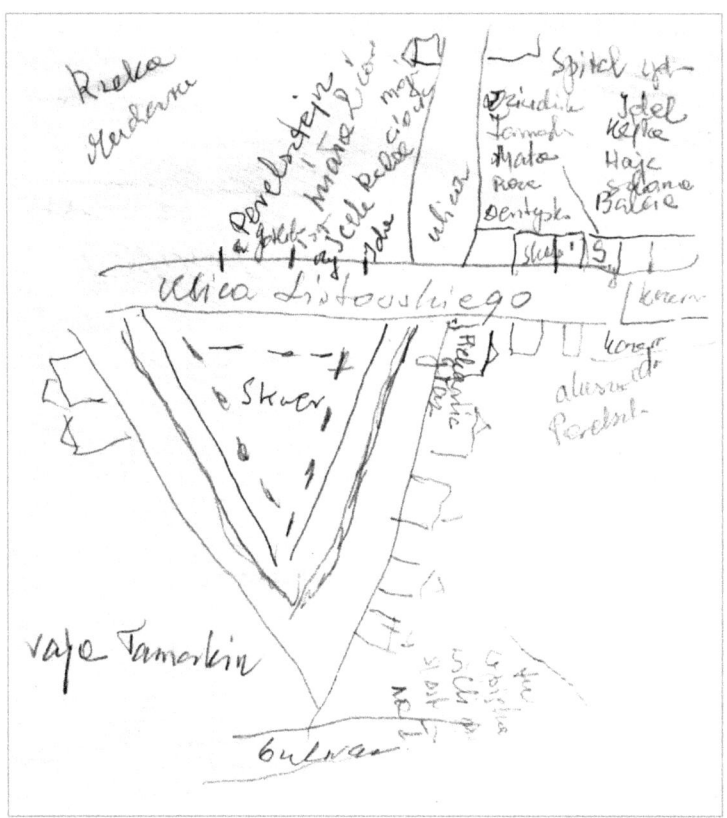

My mother was a wonderful story-teller. She could convey the atmosphere of her town and home splendidly. Based on her words, I could visualize my grandmother's kitchen, recreate the aromas of the dishes she was baking or cooking for the Sabbath, and see in my mind's eye the neighbors visiting and gossiping.

* * *

Always a very good student, my mother excelled in math. Until the war broke out, she attended a state Jewish school, where a rabbi would come to teach the children religion and where no classes were held on Saturdays. While she recalled some pogroms, and the routine throwing of stones at Jewish funeral processions by Polish boys, overall Mother claimed she had a carefree youth. Having graduated from high school (*desyatsiletka*) when Brześć was under the Soviet rule, she subsequently attended a commercial school (*gimnazium kupieckie*) and completed her studies with flying colors. Immediately afterwards, she was employed as a clerk in a jewelry store, "Yuvilertorg."

My mother's family experienced an instant deterioration of living conditions when Brześć was overtaken by the Soviets. Their house being fairly large, two families were imposed on them as tenants. Her sister Chaja, her husband, and their son were evicted from their own home. Still, life was tolerable for my mother—there were even moments of levity. She told me about the fun local youth had as they watched the Soviet military men bite oranges and, repelled by the taste, throw the fruit away, not realizing it had to be peeled first; or saw their wives appear in public, even at parties, wearing nightgowns. The Russian women, ignorant of local fashion rules, could not distinguish between the local night wear and day wear. Mother also remembered going to the club Buryevyestnik (so named by the Soviets) where she happened to be dancing the night before the Germans invaded the Soviet Union.

Mother got home late that night, went to bed, and was awoken by loud noises. These were the sounds of German tanks rolling into Brześć. Her life now changed most drastically. German soldiers appeared at my mother's house early the next morning. Pointing a gun at her father's head, they approached her and took her gold Star of David necklace. Mother spoke to them in German and pleaded with them to let her father go, and was successful.

My grandmother Rifka was not at home that morning; she had gone to visit Chaja in Kovel and it was not until several days later that she managed to get a ride back to Brześć in a stranger's car.

Shortly the horror—the relentless abuse, deprivations, and humiliations—began. Mother's family was forced to move to the ghetto, giving up its big house in exchange for a two-room apartment with a small garden. The looting began. Valuables were confiscated, with constant demands made that Jews part with their furniture, jewelry, and various other belongings. The Germans rounded up Jewish men and women for work, and her father and brother were recruited to do menial jobs. There were repeated threats of death to both Lejb and Szlomo. On numerous occasions, Mother interceded on her father's and brother's behalf. She saved them from deportation, and her entreaties in her fluent German initially secured them easier jobs. Both were made to work in a saw mill, but alas, they did not escape harrowing experiences later on, when both were sent to the Brześć fortress to carry out the corpses of Soviet soldiers. One day, Szlomo was locked into a room with several vicious dogs. He loved animals, and had a way of placating them, so the dogs did him no harm, but after this experience, which clearly traumatized him, his hair started falling out. My grandfather Lejb was badly bitten by a dog a German soldier sent to attack him when he saw Lejb give some bread to a Soviet prisoner. It seems that the soldier actually felt some remorse after that, because the next day he gave my grandfather some ointment to help him heal.

My mother was also sent to work. At first, she worked with her father in the saw mill, helping him arrange the cut pieces of wood. Later she was given more disturbing assignments within the ghetto. Among other tasks, she was made to clean apartments whose walls and floors were often covered with blood. Although she had no food all day, when she returned home from such tasks she could not stomach food. In no time, she developed an ulcer.

Grandmother Rifka tried to keep the family fed by cooking soups out of the few ingredients she could obtain in the ghetto, mostly nettles and potatoes. She sometimes added shredded carrots to create the appearance of a more substantive meal, and was kind enough to share her meager food supplies with beggars who routinely knocked on their door.

* * *

A few years after the war, my mother discovered some relatives who survived the war in the Soviet Union. Two of her cousins, Jankiel and Szymon Pinczuk, had returned to Poland and settled in the town of Legnica. My immediate family lived in Katowice by then. I still remember the visit of Uncle Szymon's wife, Rachela, in our Katowice apartment. I was about 8 years old and I followed her constantly, addressing her as "*Ciociu, ciociu*" (Auntie, auntie). Until then, unlike my schoolmates, I had met no relatives, and it was a thrill for me to finally have an aunt. I doubt it would have mattered to me if I had understood that she was not a blood relation, only an aunt by marriage to my mother's distant cousin.

In the early 1950s, Mother discovered yet another cousin, Szlomo (nicknamed Sioma) Nirenblat, who had survived by escaping to Tashkent and who had met and married his wife Hasia (Asia) Szochet there. Mother established contact with them and they conducted a regular correspondence. They named their first-born daughter Regina, after me. In 1956, I accompanied my mother on her first postwar foreign trip to meet these relatives. They had moved from Tashkent to Lvov in Soviet Ukraine by then, and had another child, a boy they named Leon. During our visit to Lvov, Mother succeeded in persuading her cousin Sioma to repatriate to Poland. He and his family returned to Poland and settled in Warsaw, but left for Israel shortly afterwards. My mother's other cousins, Jankiel and Szymon Pinczuk, and their families also emigrated to Israel. All of these cousins and their wives have passed away by now. In June 2011, during my brief visit to Israel, I had the good fortune to see Aunt Asia Nirenblat one last time. I am still in touch with her daughter Regina (who assumed the Hebrew name Dganit) and the children of my mother's other cousins, who reside in Israel and have children and grandchildren of their own by now.

* * *

During the Soviet occupation, my mother learned to speak Russian quite well. She also studied the language formally in Katowice after the war. Having completed a three-year special program for teachers, she initially taught adult evening classes in Silesia, and later taught Russian in Warsaw high schools. Mother gained great recognition as a teacher. Indeed, she had an innate talent to make her classes come alive. She included jokes, poems, and fairy tales in her teaching, and also assorted proverbs and songs. Recognized for her superior methodology, she was often asked to impart her knowledge to teachers in other schools, and received a state award for her excellence in teaching. Another honor bestowed on her was a gold medal (*złota oznaka honorowa*) from the Society of Polish-Soviet Friendship for "promoting friendship among the nations." I should also mention that in 1948 she received the Medal of Valor—*Krzyż walecznych*—for her wartime underground activities, and in 1966 a special certificate of recognition for her activities in promoting the celebration of the one thousandth

Chapter Ten | Mother and Her Family

Mother's teacher ID from Warsaw

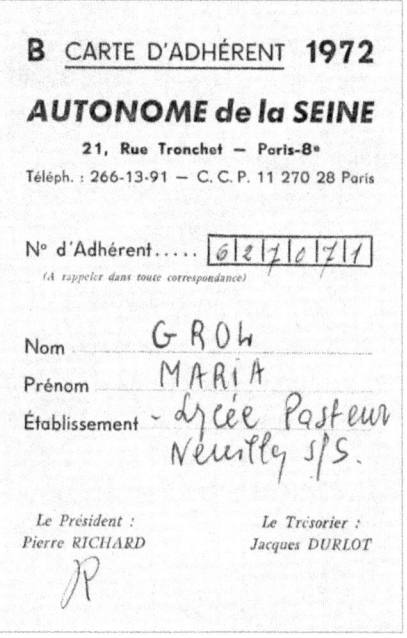

Mother's French Teacher ID

anniversary of the Polish nation (*za działalność społeczną w obchodach tysiąclecia państwa polskiego*).)

Her knowledge of Russian turned out to be useful for my mother in France as well, and she obtained jobs as a teacher's assistant in two Parisian high schools. The last school where she taught, and from which she retired in 1987, was the suburban Lycée Pasteur in Neuilly-sur-Seine.

* * *

Married for 56 years, Mother claimed that Father was the only man in her life. While there were tense moments in their relationship, especially during the debates about moving to Israel and returning from Israel to Poland, and those concerning subsequent moves and migrations, on the whole my parents had a very solid relationship. Mother was always sensitive to my father's needs. She took good care of him, ensuring that he had peace and quiet when he wrote, preparing special meals for him when he was sick, and practically absolving him of any domestic chores.

Even in her old age, Mother could not be accused of being self-absorbed, as some elderly people become. In fact, all her life Mother was an exceedingly altruistic and generous person. I remember the joy with which she would bring me a few tiny tomatoes when I was little. She knew I liked tomatoes, and in the postwar years in Poland these were generally available only in the summer. When occasionally hothouse tomatoes appeared in the stores in the spring, she would run and buy them for me, even though they were very expensive. I can also recall other parental sacrifices she made when I was a child. For example, she would purchase clothing for me when her own wardrobe was minimal. I remember her taking her skirts to a dressmaker to have them turned inside out when the fabric became shiny from excessive wear—for rather than treat herself to new garments, she bought clothing for me. (I tried to reciprocate as soon as I could: with my very first paycheck I bought a winter coat for my mother.)

Indeed, my mother's acts of generosity toward me and my children were countless. When my daughter and then my son were born, Mother came to the United States to assist me. She also visited on subsequent summer vacations and was the source of countless bedtime stories invented especially for my children. Polish was the only language she had in common with my children. I still recall my daughter's frequent request, "*Babciu, opowiedz mi straszną historię*" (Grandma, tell me a scary story). Mother always obliged her, yet moderated the scary aspect, occasionally provoking my daughter's frustration. Her love for me, my sister, and our children was truly unconditional.

Mother's innate generosity extended to neighbors and friends as well. Whenever she visited anyone, she always came bearing gifts. I also recall an incident in Paris indicative of my Mother's sensitivity and magnanimity. We were walking in her neighborhood, the 14th Arrondissement. The street was quite deserted at the time, and I suddenly noticed some rolled banknotes by the curb and picked them up. It was a sum of about 60 francs. My mother instantly began expressing compassion for the person who had lost the money. For several days her heart went out to that person. I imagine that many people would have focused on the windfall, rather

Chapter Ten | Mother and Her Family

than the one who lost the money. Not my Mother. For days she brought up the topic, expressing sadness and empathy each time.

Another act of generosity was the donation of her body to science. She had told me that she intended to do so, but I was not certain if she had actually arranged it. However, among the papers I sorted while clearing out her Paris apartment, I found her hand-written note with the inscription "Don du corps, 45 Rue de Saints Peres, 75016 Paris, tel: 01.42.86.20.48," and then a letter from Academie de Paris, Université René Descartes, Paris V, Centre du Don Des Corps, at the above address, thanking my mother for her "generous initiative."

When I was in my late teens, Mother was taller than me by at least seven inches. In some of our early pictures, it is clear that she towered over me. Then gradually, due to osteoporosis, she started to shrink. In the final years of her life she was a slightly bent, frail woman considerably shorter than me.

Sadly, Mother's final years were lonely. She became a widow in 1999. On one of my last visits to Paris, I looked at the address book by her phone, and about 70 names were crossed out: her friends and acquaintances were dying, and she became increasingly socially isolated. There was only one friend in Paris and one other person, the wife of my father's cousin, to whom she could talk in Yiddish, the language of her childhood, which was closest to her heart. While she spent the summers with my sister in Italy, most of the year she stayed in Paris alone.

Mother's physical needs were certainly met in Paris. She had a lovely apartment. She lived practically across the street from a hospital and had excellent medical care and other social services. A cleaning lady provided by the city visited her regularly. She had the option of lavish lunches at a nearby senior citizens' center and often ventured there. A social worker checked on her regularly, and yet my mother was lonely.

I called her often, wrote her frequent letters, and visited her whenever I could, but much as I tried to counteract her isolation, I could not. I ended up living in a country where health insurance for my mother, given her assorted prior conditions, was virtually impossible. For over thirty years, I had a tenured position in Buffalo, New York, and if Mother had moved to be with us she would not only have had to endure long winters, but she would have lost much of her cherished independence, since she could not drive or speak English. Moreover, for many years we lived in different countries, and our frames of reference with regard to lifestyle grew distinctly divergent. After my mother left Brześć, her sense of "homelessness" never entirely left her, but she felt more at home in Europe: America frightened her.

* * *

Two German men—Hermann Meyer and Dr. Schelenberg—helped my mother survive the war, and so did two Polish women—the shopkeeper in Brześć and the Bialystok landlady. Their actions should have restored my mother's faith in humanity, but they did not, or at least not fully. She remained distrustful of people and, particularly after 1968, her attitude toward Poles fluctuated. I cannot forget the remark she made to me some 20 years ago in France, after we overheard an antisemitic remark made in Polish: "*Jak zobaczysz Polaka przechodź na drugą stronę ulicy*" (When you see a Pole, go over to the other side of the street). And yet she had a long-lasting friendship with her reactionary Polish neighbor, showering her with affection and gifts. Their relationship puzzled me for years, and upon Mom's death I felt compelled to write about it. (That essay is included here as the chapter "Danuta").

When I was already in my forties, Mother revealed to me that she felt guilty about telling me of her wartime experiences when I was so young, and for having made me her confidant throughout her life. I must admit that there were occasional moments when it was a burden, and when her reactions and her perceptions of people or events struck me as affected by her Holocaust traumas. I cannot forget, for instance, the look of fear and tension in her eyes when she accompanied me to the Orly airport in Paris and suddenly there was an announcement over the loudspeaker that a suspicious package had been found. Passengers were asked to evacuate the waiting area. I suppose that most people would be frightened under such circumstances, and one could observe signs of anxiety and apprehension in their faces, but my Mother's face reflected deep-seated and indescribable horror. Certain things from the past one can recall in photographic detail, and this happens to be one of those scenes for me—my mother's look was stamped with a fearsome dread. I could see in her eyes a response much stronger than what the potential current threat called for.

I never admitted to my mother my occasional "Holocaust fatigue," and to this day I am grateful to her both for her unconditional love and for connecting me with the past generations. Also, as with age I became more skeptical myself, I came to the conclusion that perhaps many of Mother's reactions were justified.

From my current perspective, I understand my mother much better. Pitched into a world of fear during the war, experiencing degradation as a Jew and relentless anxiety when pretending to be Aryan, she was repeatedly challenged to retain her sanity. She lost her family, her community, and her way of life, yet she engaged in a lifelong battle to regain a sense of normalcy—and she prevailed. Mother's internal exile and life-altering

My mother in her Paris apartment, displaying poems dedicated to her. On the left, a poem written in French by my daughter Hanna; on the right, a birthday poem in Polish, an acrostic, written by me. (2002)

geographic migrations undoubtedly left their mark, but her responses were not psychotic. I'm sure that growing up she never imagined the existential predicaments that awaited her and the challenges her life would present. She certainly never expected that she would have to leave her native town and become a "wandering Jew"; that her children as well would live in several countries and move repeatedly (more than 20 times in my case); that there would be linguistic barriers in her communication with her own grandchildren. She had to develop different ways of emotional and geographic anchoring. And for me, too, the challenge of anchoring remains, and the notion of home continues to be fluid.

* * *

Alas, neither my mother nor my father was able to salvage any pictures of their relatives. In fact, Mother had to destroy the few she took out of the Brześć ghetto, fearful that if they were found her "Aryan" cover would be blown. To this day, other than my parents' verbal descriptions, I have no idea what my grandmothers looked like, nor my Aunt Chaja—who was reputed to have been a beauty—nor my uncle Marek, my father's younger brother, or any other relative. Yet, unlike the "vacuum" and questions I still have regarding most of my father's family, when it comes to Mother's relatives I managed to obtain various external confirmations of their existences and activities. Lejb Pinczuk and Malkil Pinczuk (Chaja's husband), as well as his mother Cypa Pomeraniec, for example, are all listed as merchants in the 1937 Taxpayers list I discovered online.[4]

I also located the pictures of three generations of the males in the Pinczuk family, which I have included below. Initially, I discovered only the picture of my maternal great-grandfather Mojsze Pinczuk in two albums of photographs published after the war.[5] I was thrilled at the discovery, and so was my mother, although she objected to the fact that the inscription under the picture was inaccurate. Mother claimed that her grandfather was the founder of the Wysokie Litewskie synagogue, not just its *gabbai*. Incidentally, when I visited the Jewish Museum in Berlin in the spring of 2002, to my surprise, a temporary exhibit featured the same photograph. For years this was the only pre-war picture of a relative I had; until I was in my sixties I saw no other. Then, a year ago, I discovered pictures of my maternal grandfather Lejb Pinczuk and my uncle Shlomo Pinczuk, as well as a picture of my mother at the age of 21, which is included in Chapter 1, in the Yad Vashem archive. These identity card photographs were taken during the Soviet occupation of Brześć, and I was thrilled to find them. These pictures are my special connection to the world of my perished family. Given the absence in my life of any relatives of the generations preceding my parents, I viewed these photographs as priceless links with the past, yet I also came to the sad realization that essentially they document my loss.

---

[4] http://www.brest-belarus.or/rd/tax1937/Brest1937taxpayers_P.i.html

[5] The first volume in which the picture appeared is Lucjan Dobroszycki and Barbara Kirshenblatt Gimblett, eds., *Image Before My Eyes: A Photographic History of Jewish Life in Poland 1864-1934* (New York: Schocken, 1977). The second album which included the picture is *POLYN: Jewish Life in the Old Country: Alter Kacyzne*, 136.

Chapter Ten | Mother and Her Family

Mojsze Pinczuk, my maternal great-grandfather, 1921 (photo by Alter Kacyzne, courtesy of YIVO and the Forward Association, Inc.)

Lejb Pinczuk
(my maternal grandfather, 1940).
Picture from the Yad Vashem Archive

Szlomo Pinczuk
(my mother's older brother, 1940).
Picture from the Yad Vashem Archive

Chapter Eleven

Danuta

My parents, as will be recalled, came to France as refugees from Poland at the end of 1969. Initially, they rented a small flat on Boulevard Brune, in the 14th Arrandissement, but a few months later they moved to a 16th-floor apartment on a nearby street with a splendid view of the Eiffel Tower. I liked the view, and the ambience of their quarter, not to mention the pampering and affection they showered on my children and me during our visits. Yet there was a persistent irritant during each of my stays: the sudden appearances of a nosy neighbor. Whenever I came to see my parents in Paris, I would also—inescapably—see Danuta (not her real name), who resided in the same high-rise, and had a habit of showing up uninvited.

Although she was exactly my age, we seemed to have little in common, and I rarely found conversations with her interesting. Yet I felt I had to make concessions. Although Paris beckoned and time spent with my parents was precious, I engaged in trivial chitchat with her so as not to be rude. Danuta's intrusions regularly marred my otherwise lovely visits.

For more than thirty years, Danuta was my mother's neighbor. I was perpetually puzzled by the nature of their relationship. I ascribed their frequent contact to the loneliness of the two women, both emigres, both rather uncomfortable in the French culture, both tossed to Paris by an accident of fate. Danuta became a "Parisienne" by marriage when she was whisked from a village in Poland by a Frenchman of Polish extraction who lured her with false promises of riches. My parents, of cousre, left Warsaw in the aftermath of the Polish government's ugly antisemitic campaign of 1968.

Chapter Eleven | Danuta

I could not understand why my parents put up with Danuta's company. They had quite a few other friends, so why her, I marveled. What did they, Jewish intellectuals, liberal and honest to a fault, have in common with Danuta—bigoted, antisemitic, simple-minded, quarrelsome, and dishonest? She stole from her employers and bragged about it. She used ethnic slurs in her comments about her Jewish bosses and, many years into their friendship, revealed to my mother that she had voted for Jean-Marie le Pen, the fascist candidate for the presidency of France. My father had passed away by then. I doubt that he would have tolerated Danuta's presence under his roof after such an admission—in fact, I am convinced that's where he would have drawn the line. But my mother continued to condone her visits.

If one needed any additional evidence of Danuta's antisemitism, her own mother provided it. On her several visits to Paris, her mother divulged to mine Danuta's "pronouncements" that hit even closer home. For example, Danuta allegedly envied my mother her bigger apartment, and referred to her as "*ta żydówa*" (that kike) behind my mother's back.

My mother overlooked that, too. Perhaps, given that she knew of Danuta's tense and troubled relationship with her parents, my mother chose not to believe these denunciations. Yet she retained them in her memory, and years later told me about them, so the disclosures must have been hurtful.

Despite Danuta's many very objectionable qualities, she grew to be more than merely a neighbor: she became my mother's substitute daughter and a repository of our family's stories. My mother, in turn, became Danuta's surrogate parent and, primarily, a shoulder to cry on. One might even say she became Danuta's "Wailing Wall." Mother was repeatedly called upon to listen patiently to Danuta's tales of woe about fights with her husband, her mother, or her brother; her discovery that she was an illegitimate child; or her troubles with her two sons. For years my mother would open her doors and her heart to Danuta, console her, cheer her up, give her presents, and regularly dispense advice on diverse subjects, from fashion to finance, and—repeatedly—offer suggestions on ways to maintain peace of mind and peace at home.

I have to acknowledge that Danuta reciprocated by rendering Mother some favors. She forwarded the mail whenever Mother left town for extended periods of time, mostly to visit my sister in Italy. On several occasions, when Mother was already elderly and frail, Danuta accompanied her to the railway station to help her board a train and place her luggage on a shelf. She also patiently listened to Mother's stories, even when, as Mother aged, they became repetitious. Even then, though, I did not give Danuta credit for her kindness. I believed—cynical as my bent of mind was—that she listened because Mother's apartment was a place of refuge, preferable to her own home, where turmoil was the rule.

After my father passed away in 1999, Mother refused to consider relocation, or, as she put it, "further transplantations." (She found America too daunting, and Italy too chaotic.) I felt particularly sorry for my mother then, sorry that she had ended up living in Paris alone, with my sister and me hundreds or thousands of miles away. I presumed that, as an elderly and lonely emigre, she was forced by necessity to accept Danuta's presence in her life. I still viewed their relationship with great ambivalence, for, despite Danuta's crassness, their contacts continued. Over and over again, I was amazed by my mother's tolerance. When in late May of 2004 my mother left for her annual visit to Italy—the last one, as it turned out—it was once again Danuta who was entrusted with the key to Mother's apartment and with forwarding her mail.

Shortly after my mother's funeral in Italy, when I went to Paris to face the most unpleasant task of clearing out my parents' apartment, Danuta turned up repeatedly. She would drop by, out of the blue as usual, and interfere with my sorting, packing, and reviewing of papers and documents—that is, with all the chores I had to complete under a tremendous time pressure. While I was reluctant to accept her offers of help, she was relentless in reiterating them. At first I suspected her of calculated niceness, as she stood to receive many things from my parents' apartment, but I had to change my mind, and once I allowed her to, she actually ended up being quite helpful in dealing with the building administration and in demystifying the workings of local bureaucracies.

Moreover, she told me stories I had never heard before about the beginning of her friendship with my mother. She recalled how they met in the street when they were both relative newcomers to France; how Mother approached her, hearing Danuta speak Polish to her little son; how their accidental street encounters became more frequent; how Mother, who had contemplated moving into a different neighborhood, ultimately opted for the building where Danuta lived, despite its proximity to a railway track.

I listened to these tales eagerly, for they made me feel my mother's presence when she was already gone. Yet Danuta's account of my mother's last phone call from Italy, when—she told me—Mother had asked to be met at the train station and Danuta had dissuaded her from coming back to Paris so soon, disturbed me. In my mind I questioned Danuta's motives again. Entrusted with the keys to my mother's apartment, did Danuta want to have it all to herself a bit longer? Did she try to postpone Mother's return for selfish and self-serving reasons?

In late August, on the day I was leaving France, Danuta dropped by again. She looked wistfully at the empty apartment and was not the chatterbox she had tended to be on previous occasions. She seemed unusually pensive. Her voice was breaking as she spoke of her real sense of loss, and she could not hold back her tears. I was genuinely surprised by her emotional outburst, by her sobbing and her very apparent grief. Her tears moved me deeply. The fact that a woman of Danuta's ilk, so rough on the edges and so bigoted, could cry profusely over my Jewish mother's passing made me see the neighbor in a different light. It also made me acknowledge what an exceptional human being my mother had been, to elicit such grief. I grew to appreciate even more Mother's rare generosity of spirit.

I also understood more, now, how deeply Danuta had cared for my mother. Clearly this was a more complex relationship than I had been willing to realize. Upon my return to the United States, I wrote to Danuta, expressing my gratitude for her many years of friendship with my mother. I understood at long last that while I loved my mother dearly, called her often, wrote regularly, and visited whenever I could, Danuta was physically there when I could not be; that she and Mother had become close in ways not apparent to me for years; that despite all appearances to the contrary, despite my contempt and ambivalence, Danuta's presence in my mother's life may well have been a gift. Perhaps it was a less than perfect gift, but it was a gift nevertheless. I consider her weeping a testimonial to my mother's magnanimity and count it, along with an Italian grave-digger's gesture of putting a single rose on my mother's coffin, among the very touching farewells honoring my mother.

Chapter Twelve

On Graves, Burial Rites, and the Search for Identity

The burial of one's ancestors is a sacred obligation. It is "a right and a rite," as Seamus Heaney, the 1995 Nobel laureate in literature, declared.[1] Victims of the Holocaust have been deprived of both their rites and their rights. Whether they went up in smoke in crematoria, starved in ghettoes, died during death marches, or were shot and buried in unmarked mass graves, the consequence is that most of their survivors and descendants have no graves to visit.

Part of the legacy of the Holocaust is the constant—conscious or subconscious—mourning for the dead, and as a result of the Holocaust as well as the post-Holocaust upheavals, there is a sense of dispersion and concomitantly uprootedness. Most survivors and their children, I believe, are thus affected.

To bury one's ancestors or relatives and have access to their graves are profoundly human needs addressed in the Old Testament (e.g., in the book of Genesis in connection with the burial of Sarah, Isaac, Jacob, and Joseph) and expressed in many literary works throughout history, from Sophocles' *Antigone* to Adam Mickiewicz's *Dziady* (Forefathers' Eve). All Saints' Day is solemnly observed throughout Europe by visits to the graves of family members. During the ten days that come between Rosh Hashana and Yom Kippur, it is the custom of some Jews to pray beside the graves of their relatives.[2] Others attend Yorzeit and Yizkor services and light

---

[1] In a National Public Radio interview with the poet, following the publication of his translation of *The Burial of Thebes* (aired on Nov.8, 2004).

[2] See a description of the ritual in Rebecca Goldstein's novel *Mazel* (New York: Viking, 1995), 129.

memorial candles. To this day, thousands of Hassidim flock to Poland to visit the graves of spiritual leaders who passed away prior to the Holocaust. Visitation of graves and rites related to commemoration of the dead are an inherent part of most, if not all, cultures.

In her book *Holocaust and Memory*, Barbara Engelking quotes a survivor who expressed the traditional view regarding the significance of graves:

> I think that life is a parade of generations, a relay of generations. After all, when we talk about our mother country, we are thinking among other things of graves. The remains of our ancestors are in this earth. A person has to remember those who've passed on.[3]

Indeed, the same interviewee—Edward—relates patriotism to the location of graves:

> A mother country is not such a complicated thing: it's the earth where my roots have been put down, where I was born and where my grave—where someone might light a candle—will be.[4]

To be deprived of that sense of rootedness causes psychological distress. The psychologist Bruno Bettelheim has written extensively about survivors' guilt and the related experiencing of inconsolable mourning. He stresses that

> … cultural patterns like the funeral, the manner, time and place of carrying out mourning, created a special ritual of saying farewell to the dead. The time of visiting graves, the time of recollecting, helps us to come to terms with the death of those close to us. It is however difficult to come to terms with death when we cannot experience mourning fully because it has no beginning and no end—when the date of death is unknown, when there is no grave, when there is no community of people who also knew and loved those dear to us, and with whom we would be able to recollect them. It is impossible to part with the dead who have not been mourned.[5]

---

[3] After Barbara Engelking, *Holocaust and Memory: The Experience of the Holocaust and Its Consequences: An Investigation Based on Personal Narratives*, ed. Gunnar S. Paulsson, trans. Emma Harris (London: Leicester University Press, 2001), 249.

[4] Ibid., 262

[5] Ibid., 248-9.

As most survivors have no knowledge of the locations of their murdered relatives' graves, their mourning had to assume different forms. Samuel Pisar, a child survivor of Majdanek, Auschwitz, and Dachau who wrote the new lyrics to Leonard Bernstein's "Kaddish" Symphony No. 3, claimed that his words were a memorial to his lost family. As he put it, "My memory is the only tomb they have."[6] He was echoing Elie Wiesel, who on numerous occasions has stated that the victims of the Holocaust have no physical cemeteries and that the survivors are their cemeteries.

Many survivors who were children during the Holocaust kept quiet for decades, yet felt compelled late in their lives to write about their perished families. Why? To quote M. Michael Thaler, "The question: Why now? is asked and answered by the witnesses themselves: a growing and undeniable need to leave behind a memorial 'to my dearest ones, who do not even have a grave' (*bo chcę zostawić wspomnienie o moich najdroższych, którzy nie mają nawet mogił*)."[7]

Not all survivors were able to sublimate their pain into artistic forms, but all have internalized it, I believe, and to a lesser or greater extent, on some level and in some form, they have passed on their mourning and pain to the next generations.

* * *

Most children of Holocaust survivors were deprived not only of ancestral graves, but also of extended families. That affected their relationships with their parents by intensifying them. Some children had to compete with the ghosts of older siblings who had perished in the Shoah. After the war, many children were taught harsh existential lessons. Note, for instance, Janina Katz's account:

> *Ojciec nauczył mnie, że pytanie, które tak często się słyszy: "Co chcesz zrobić ze swoim życiem?", to pytanie luksusowe. W naszym przypadku*

---

[6] Samuel Pisar, quoted in Steven Erlanger, "After Survival, A Journey to Self-Recovery," *The New York Times International* (July 11, 2009): A8.

[7] M. Michel Thaler, "Unlikely Witnesses: Children's Voices and What They Tell Us about the Holocaust Experience" in *The Legacy of the Holocaust: Children and the Holocaust*, ed. Zygmunt Mazur et al. (Kraków: Jagiellonian University Press, 2002).

odpowiedź brzmiała "przeżyć je." Albo: "Umrzeć, nim dam komuś szansę zabicia mnie, nim rozkażą mi pić własny mocz i jeść własne gówno."[8]

(Father taught me that the question, which one hears so often: "What do you want to do with your life?" is a luxury question. In our case the answer was: "To survive." Or: "To die before I give someone a chance to kill me, before they order me to drink my own urine and to eat my own excrement.)

Children of survivors were inescapably saddled with the burden of sharing in their parents' grief—whether the parents expressed that grief explicitly or not. The children were expected (again whether this was expressed or not) to compensate for the Holocaust losses, to provide vicarious satisfaction to the parents and placate the parents' need for vindication and reaffirmation of life. All of this is documented by now in many memoirs, academic studies, and literary works written in several countries and in several languages. The inconsolable mourning has been transmuted by children of the Holocaust survivors in a variety of ways and is clearly reflected in their own writings and lives.

To be sure, while the Holocaust was and continues to be a legacy to be dealt with, and while all children of survivors have been affected by it in some way, their responses to the calamity of Shoah are quite diverse. Some children of survivors deliberately reject the legacy; others minimize it; and some chafe under its burden. Still, many become "memorial candles," to use Dina Wardi's term.

In Wardi's 1992 book *Memorial Candles: Children of the Holocaust*, the Israeli psychotherapist, who has worked extensively with groups of children of Holocaust survivors, claimed that in every survivor's family one child is chosen as the instrument of commemoration, devotion, and mourning. According to the writer Eva Hoffman, whose many accomplishments include psychoanalytical training, "[o]nce such a symbolic role is conferred on them [i.e., the role of a "memorial candle"], the children rarely have the wherewithal to refuse it. They become votaries on the altar of Shoah, their own lives and selves dedicated to their hurt parents and to the perished."[9]

---

[8] Janina Katz, "Abram (fragment powieści)," *Odra*, No.5, vol. XLIX (May 2009): 9.

[9] Hoffman, Eva. *After Such Knowledge: Memory, History and the Legacy of the Holocaust: Where Memory of the Holocaust Ends and History Begins* (New York: Public Affairs, 2004), 64.

Indeed, so emotionally involved with their parents have some of those children become that many never, or very late, come to the conclusion that their own lives have any significance.

Indeed, most children of survivors appointed as "memorial candles" experience sorrow and on some level share the history of their parents' pain. In one way or another the post-Holocaust generation, as Arthur Cohen put it, "bears the scars without the wounds."[10] Yet the degree to which they experience the sorrow and the attitudes they assume vary widely.

Bożena Keff in her book *Utwór o matce i ojczyźnie* (An Opus About a Mother and the Fatherland), published in Kraków, Poland, in 2008, expressed simmering anger about the gloom imposed on her and the transfer of the trauma to her, and for having had to live under the toxic, dark cloud of the Holocaust all her life. The work was described by one critic as "a cross of an opera, tragedy and oratorium" in which "a lofty lament mixes with vulgar outpourings (z *ordynarnym bluzgiem*)."[11]

In this clearly autobiographical work, the character of the daughter feels ignored and diminished by the mother, her own experiences made less relevant than the mother's. More than that, she feels deprived of entitlement to the family history. The mother is presented as an oppressive and demanding parasite whom the daughter feels helpless to resist. Note the following excerpt:

"A skoro masz takie pretensje i skoro ci nie odpowiadam jako twoja Matka, To mnie zabij. Proszę!"

(Well, if you have such complaints and I don't suit you as your Mother, then kill me. Please!)

In response, the daughter's thoughts are:

Zabić cię, [...] jak cię nie zabili Niemcy, dwie armie przynajmniej, dywizje pancerne, czołgi i lotnictwo. Całe cztery lata, to ja mam dać radę?

(Kill you, [...] the Germans didn't kill you, at least two armies didn't, armored divisions, tanks, and the air force. Over the entire four years they didn't, so how can I manage it?)[12]

---

[10] Arthur Cohen, *The Tremendum* (New York: Crossroad, 1981), 2.
[11] Przemyslaw Czaplinski, "Mausoleum," *Tygodnik Powszechny* (September 9, 2008), online.
[12] Bożena Keff, *Utwór o Matce i Ojczyżnie* (Kraków: Korporacja ha!art, 2008), 57. My translation. R.G.

Indeed, the daughter resorts to very offensive personal diatribes and vulgar curses several times. She refers to the mother as "*Głucha jak hiena*" (deaf as a hyena, p. 39), and explodes at one point, " *Udław się egotyczna ślepa kretynko gwałcicielko pizdo!*" (Choke, you egotistical blind cretin rapist cunt!).

The process of writing the book must have been cathartic and therapeutic for the author. In this original poetic and somewhat surrealistic work, Bozena Keff released a great deal of pent-up resentments. It is an exceptionally honest and bold work, reflecting the daughter's struggle for her own identity, for the sense of entitlement to her own life, for the right to exit the trap of Shoah. I must confess, however, that I wondered whether the reader should not be spared some of the most emotional, though often poeticized, "outpourings." Portions of the book are likely to appall some readers, and must have appalled Keff's mother, who who was still alive when the book was published. In essence, the mother, a Holocaust survivor, is presented—to put it bluntly—as a monster strangling the daughter and poisoning her life.

Another, much better known, example of a "memorial candle" is Art Spiegelman. While in his graphic novel *Maus: A Survivor's Tale*[13] the central narrator is the father, it is clear that the trauma of the Holocaust was passed on to the son, and the novel charts in detail the troubled father/son relationship.

In Eva Hoffman's play "The Ceremony," which though unpublished so far has had several public readings, one finds reflected a broader gamut of emotions, ranging from resentment for having been haunted by the secondary memories of Shoah, through a variety of ambivalent feelings, to compassion and total identification with the victims. The play considers the response to the Jedwabne affair, i.e., the herding into a barn and burning of hundreds of Jews by their Christian neighbors in the Polish village of Jedwabne, a World War II incident brought to public attention by Jan Gross's book *The Neighbors*.

To the category of compassionate "memorial candles" belongs Helen Epstein, the keynote speaker at the Legacy of the Holocaust conference held in Cracow in 2007, and the author of a loving book about her mother

---

[13] New York: Pantheon, 1986.

titled *Where She Came From: A Daughter's Search for Her Mother's History*.[14] She has also published *Children of the Holocaust: Conversations with Sons and Daughters of Survivors*,[15] which contains additional testimonials of "memorial candles." Professor Ronald J. Berger, the author of *Constructing a Collective Memory of the Holocaust: A Life Story of Two Brothers' Survival*,[16] can also be qualified as a very sympathetic "memorial candle" by choice. So may I.

I feel a sense of moral obligation to write about my parents' experiences. I consider it my "sacred mission," since I don't want my parents—and by extension any of the Holocaust victims—to fall out of history. I identify myself both as a conveyor of the voice of the real witnesses (i.e., my parents) and a mix of an intellectual and personal affective link with the past. I would consider silence a dereliction of my duty.

Elie Wiesel was certainly right when he wrote in his book *A Jew Today*[17] that "it was easier for a prisoner to imagine himself free in Auschwitz, than it would be for you to imagine yourself a prisoner there."[18] I suspect the imaginations of most of his readers, including myself, are indeed subject to such limitations. Yet while I occasionally question the range of my imagination and the value of my testimony, being "a secondary," or "once removed" witness, and question as well my ability to be critical and objective, I cannot *not* do it. I share Sanford Pinsker's belief that "it is silence that may, finally, be the unforgivable crime of those who could have spoken but who did not."[19]

I am deeply disturbed when I see the Holocaust trivialized or misrepresented, let alone denied; when I see texts or films that fail on counts of both representation and presentation. Even the mispronunciation of names of camps or localities where horrors occurred, or distortions of

---

[14] New York: Holmes and Meier, 1997.

[15] New York: Penguin, 1979.

[16] Boulder: University of Colorado Press, 1995.

[17] New York: Vintage, 1979.

[18] Wiesel, 234.

[19] Sanford Pinsker in his preface to Sanford Pinsker and Jack Fischel, eds., *Literature, the Arts and the Holocaust* (Holocaust Studies Annual, vol. III, Greenwood, FL: The Penkevill Publishing Company, 2001).

Chapter Twelve | On Graves, Burial Rites, and the Search for Identity

names related to the Shoah, bother me deeply because I know it will get even worse with the passage of time: we all know the predictable dulling of memory. That is also a reason which compels me to leave a record.

* * *

Those who become "memorial candles" convey their painful legacy in a variety of ways, even by leaving cryptic records of their parents' lives on gravestones (*matzevot*). My friend Irena Janicka-Powell, whose father had died in Germany and whose mother happened to pass away in Oxford, England, had these words engraved on her mother's headstone:

> Sara Julia Janicka
> Nee Sara Rubinstein
> born Tartakov, Poland 5.6.1911
> died Oxford 2.5.2005
> Holocaust survivor
> Mother who in the midst of death
> Saved the life of her infant daughter
> We promise we shall not forget
> In grief and with love
> Your daughter Irena
> And family Brian, Adam, Robin.

This terse public testimonial will be augmented by a book Irena is writing.

The émigré poet Anna Frajlich, who currently teaches Polish literature at Columbia University and who published a number of poems concerning her family's Holocaust experiences, gave a very moving eulogy during the burial of her father at a New York City cemetery, expounding on the point that at long last she feels rooted in America because she finally has a grave to visit.

A short as-yet unpublished poem by Anna Frajlich, titled "Eva's Tree," conveys the drive toward rootedness in a very poignant way:

> For the roots
> of her genealogical tree
> Eva is looking tirelessly
> One root is stuck in Wyszogrod
> Another reached as far as Lvov
> Stubbornly she sifts in the ashes

– not everything has burned – she exclaims
Step by step
in darkness
amidst shadows
from the buds to the branches
along the trunk
Eva is reaching
Reaching for roots….[20]

Drzewo Ewy
Korzeni
genealogicznego drzewa
wytrwale szuka Ewa
jeden korzeń tkwi w Wyszogrodzie
drugi aż do Lwowa dochodzi
z uporem przebiera w popiołach
– nie wszystko spłonęło – woła
krok po kroku
w ciemnościach
wśród cieni
od pąków do gałęzi
wzdłuż pnia
sięga Ewa
sięga korzeni ….

Frajlich's poem about her cousin's search for roots reflects a very common phenomenon. Numerous children of Holocaust survivors are engaged in such projects, i.e., writing books about their parents, searching for family members, or delving into genealogical research. These assiduous undertakings are prompted by a need for anchoring and are closely bound with a search for one's own identity.

Marianne Hirsch's study *Family Frames: Photography, Narrative and Postmemory*[21] is but one example of a book documenting the emotional investment of those collecting artifacts, pictures, and stories, and re-narrating the events of the Holocaust, subjectively and emotionally investing

---

[20] My translation. R.G.
[21] Cambridge, MA: Harvard University Press, 1997.

themselves in these events and identifying themselves with incidents they have not witnessed. The Polish writer Agata Tuszyńska's works (e.g., her poetry volume titled *Łęczyca*) are other examples, and many more could be adduced.

As is commonly acknowledged now in the field of Holocaust studies, such "postmemory" is typical of the generation born in the late 1940s. The materiality of memory appears to be crucial for the survivors' children's quest for identity. A literary as well as visual tradition has emerged from this quest. Creating artworks about the dead or just recording their stories in some form is a way of honoring them and a step toward closure. Many have recognized that, and there are numerous testimonies already published or being prepared for publication, or just being written to be left as documents for the next generation. These become the expressions of mourning, and substitute graves in the absence of tangible ones. Sometimes these texts contain expressions of resentment by children of survivors whose parents couldn't or wouldn't tell them about their Holocaust experiences.

* * *

In addition to the deeper psychological turmoil, the often-inherited existential loneliness that affected many of the children of survivors, and the complicated search for identity, some children of survivors have already had to face—and the others will inevitably have to confront—the deaths of their parents. They will have to deal with painful practical considerations such as how and where to bury their parents.

The burial of relatives in the post-Holocaust era is not always a simple matter; emigration and the dispersion of families often make it a very complex challenge. Janina Katz included these heartrending words in her probably autobiographical novel *Abram*:

> *Bardzo rzadko płaczę, a jeśli płaczę, to nie z powodu mojego syna, lecz dlatego, że ojciec umarł w samotności, beze mnie. Pochowano go, rzecz jasna, zgodnie z rytuałem, ale trzeba było wynająć obcych mężczyzn, żeby ich było tylu, ile potrzeba do minianu.*
>
> (I cry very rarely, but if I cry, it's not because of my son, but because my father died alone, without me. He was buried, of course, according to ritual, but strangers had to be hired to have enough men for the *minyan*.)[22]

---

[22] Janina Katz, "Abram."

Worse yet, some children of survivors cannot ensure ritual burials, for there are no Jewish cemeteries in many places where Jews have emigrated. Moreover, children often live far away and are unable to visit and take care of their parents' graves.

* * *

Purely historical and socio-political research rarely examines individual feelings, and useful as quantitative studies and statistical reports are, they tend to promote a sense of abstraction. I have attempted to counteract that in this volume by referring to personal accounts, literary works of an autobiographical nature, and hybrid works combining social research with personal testimony. I hope that my personal story will also contribute to the understanding of both the emotional and the practical complexities.

My parents had made provisions for their burial in Paris, France, where they had immigrated in 1969. Yet, despite their careful preparations, death caught up with both of them elsewhere. In the case of my father, non-malignant yet inoperable tumors were discovered on his brain, and after three years of being in an essentially vegetative condition under my sister's care, he passed away in Italy.

As it happened, my mother also left this world in Italy, during her routine summer visit. Unlike my father, who was unconscious in the final stages of his life, she was alert and knew what awaited her well in advance.

After burying my father at an Italian cemetery five years earlier, she knew what to expect. However, she could not have anticipated that the heavy demand for burial space would, in effect, eliminate the plot for "infidels" at the Catholic cemetery, and that a stranger's grave would be placed at the foot of my father's. Being interred at a Catholic cemetery and not even next to my father's grave, but separated from it by a grave with a huge crucifix, was definitely *not* what she would have wanted.

On a recent visit, I placed stones on my parents' graves, as is traditional. While I knew that growing flowers on graves was not part of the Jewish tradition, I was gratified to see a beautiful rosebush blooming on my father's grave, and lovely flowers planted on my mother's. I thanked the gardener for the good care taken of the graves, expressing my relief that at last my parents had found a permanent resting place. I was quickly disabused of my hopeful scenario, and informed that buying a plot at that cemetery entitled one to it for ten or fifteen years only. After that time, the grave is emptied to make room for a new corpse, and the remains are put in an urn, either to be disposed of or given to the family.[23] It disturbed me deeply to learn that my parents, unwilling globe-trotters during their lives, would also be displaced after deaths.

* * *

Dispersion and the alienation related to uprooting are not problems unique to the Jews, nor to Holocaust survivors or children of Holocaust survivors. Neither is the inability to inter one's loved ones. These are lingering problems confronted by many people all over the world, for example by the families of the *Disparidos* in Latin America and the families of the victims of the 9/11 tragedy, whose laments about the lack of remnants to bury were heard with empathy all over the world. As Alex Haley made abundantly clear, the drive to establish one's roots is also not unique to Shoah survivors and their children. His book, *Roots*, by now a classic of African-American literature, triggered an avalanche of genealogical research, which continues to this day and has found ardent participants, such as the Harvard professor Henry Louis Gates, who has produced a TV series on genealogical roots of the African-American diaspora based on DNA research. Indeed, these are universal issues, but Holocaust studies may well spearhead new avenues for confronting them. Indeed, while attending the Association for Jewish Studies conference at the University of Toronto in 2008, I discovered that the Diaspora Studies Program at that university already promotes the study of Yiddish as a tool in learning about diaspora life and ways of coping with dispersion.

The dark cloud of the Holocaust has not dissipated yet. It hangs, in particular, over the few remaining survivors, who are inescapably marked by their experience. It also hangs over their children and even the next generation, affecting their lives in insidious ways. One small bit of evidence was provided by my own daughter, who spontaneously—unprompted by anyone—named her first-born child after my aunt Chaja, who had perished

---

[23] As I have learned subsequently, the practice of vacating graves to make room for "new arrivals" is not unique to Italy. It exists in other countries, such as Belgium, as well, although the time allotment varies.

160 Chapter Twelve | On Graves, Burial Rites, and the Search for Identity

My daughter at my father's grave

in the Kovel ghetto. While the Holocaust has permeated the collective consciousness, and efforts for the preservation of graves and cemeteries have found their dedicated champions, the various dimensions of mourning and symbolic burial rites have not been fully explored yet.[24] Survivors of the Shoah and their children may well be paving the way toward grasping and confronting more subtly these universal problems.

---

[24] E.g., Monika Krajewska has done a great deal in this domain in Poland, both by publishing and teaching, and Chana and Norman L. Weinberg of Buffalo, New York, have undertaken various initiatives and launched the Poland Jewish Cemeteries Restoration Project.

Chapter Twelve | On Graves, Burial Rites, and the Search for Identity 161

My sister and me at our mother's grave

Chapter Thirteen

Poems

Walking the Streets of Warsaw

For Dad

I am walking the streets of Warsaw,
the city where you were born,
the city you've always loved
but were made to leave.
This city used to be mine, too,
and now feels so unfamiliar …
New skyscrapers dot the sky.
The underground passages befuddle.
The Palace of Culture draped in
Newsweek advertising
makes the scene surreal
(Where am I? In the West?)

I'm walking the streets of Warsaw.
You are no longer among us…
I sense being woven in mysterious ways
into the fabric of history.
Why am I here?
What am I to do here?
I listen and look for signs.
I hope my words reach you …

Warsaw, 2001

WHY?

They hate me...
Not knowing me,
they hate me.
Some don't even know they hate me.
They pass me in the street, in the store,
on the bus,
and think I'm one of them.
They hate others like me.
They spew their venom in papers, graffiti,
in jokes, and turns of phrase.
I'm their alleged enemy.
In their minds I'm devious
and dangerous—
the embodiment of evil.
Personally, they may like me.
They may even say so.
They can be charming toward me.
They may do me favors.
All that changes
the moment they find out
... I am Jewish.
Some are good at covering up their shock of discovery;
some are less skilled.
Some wish it weren't so and hope
I'm joking....
Some (I can tell ...) resent my blue eyes and blond hair
that "fooled" them.
Always unsettled by their startled or dismayed looks,
I try not to show how it hurts.
Yet inside I scream: WHY?

Warsaw, 2002

Unde bonum?

Philosophers persistently
wrestle with the question—
unde malum?
Where does evil come from?
I am obsessed by the reverse.
Where does goodness come from?

How could my Mother,
given her travails,
remain so generous of spirit,
so loving and magnanimous?
How did she,
a veteran of many forays
behind the barbed wires
of the ghetto fence,
she whose world was shuttered,
who was shot at,
who cheated death by a hair,
she who was denied bread
when starving
and pregnant with me,
how did she retain
her respect for humanity,
her indissoluble capacity to love,
her drive to carry on ?
Unde bonum ?

Chapter Thirteen | Poems

Anchored in Ether?

I keep clicking on HOME
on my computer screen.
I've clicked on it
in ten cities
in the past few months.
I have clicked on it
wherever I was.
There are many nomads like me.
We experience change
all the time.
We sense change
both internal and external ...
How can we anchor ourselves?
Is "HOME" our only home now?

Walking on Pain

I wish I could fly like a bird...
For wherever we go, we tread on pain,
layers and layers of pain.
Stepping on it seems indecent.
In city after city, country after country
blood has been spilled.
The earth has been absorbing
the abuse.

In the Holy Land
each step I took reminded me
of this steady accretion.

Walking the streets of Rome,
I thought of the many martyrs,
of the young men devoured
by lions in the coliseum.

The Umschlagplatz in Warsaw
was yet another reminder
of man's bestiality
and the mountains of humiliation,
the oceans of tears
buried under the marble monument.

The map of Europe is peppered
with sites of concentration camps.
All continents have both marked
and unmarked battlefields,
glossing over dense strata of pain.

In glorious America
we tread on disgraced earth
on the pain of the natives,
on the land taken from them,
on their burial grounds.

How conveniently we forget.
How good we've become
at ignoring the pain.
How eagerly we travel
oblivious to the pervasive
—buried and not buried—
presence of pain.

Conclusion

IT IS HARD to sing of oneness when the world is not complete,
when those who once brought wholeness to our life have gone,
and naught but memory can fill the emptiness their passing leaves behind.

But memory can tell us only what we were, in company with those we loved;
it cannot help us find what each of us, alone, must now become.
Yet no one is really alone:
those who live no more, echo still within our thoughts and words,
and what they did is part of what we have become.[1]

I have written this book late in my life, and alas, after both my parents have passed away. Many children of Holocaust survivors have published their testimonials before me. Indeed, their texts have become the basis for a new field of research. Both their autobiographical writings and their experiences transmuted into literary texts or other works of art form a substantial body of knowledge which has been subjected to scrutiny and rigorous academic criticism.

Holocaust studies is a major interdisciplinary field of study by now, with various distinct "sub-divisions" continually affected by new critical trends. Courses in Holocaust studies are offered at universities in several countries. Recently, the first international master's program in Holocaust studies was launched at Haifa University in Israel. Commemorative events related to Shoah abound, and the United Nations organization declared January 23, 2013, the 68th anniversary of the liberation of Auschwitz, an International Day of Commemoration in memory of the victims of the Holocaust. There

---

[1] *Mishkan T'filah: A Reform Sidur* (New York: Central Conference of American Rabbis, 2007), 595.

are also various civic organizations promoting the study of Shoah and its aftereffects year-round, such as the impressively active organization *Drugie pokolenie* (Second Generation) in Poland.

In fact, the name of that organization stems from the new terminology that has emerged in the field of Holocaust Studies. "Second Generation" refers to children of Holocaust survivors, but there is already a "Third Generation," i.e., those who heard accounts of the Holocaust from their grandparents. The latter have also become quite vocal and active in sharing their knowledge of the Holocaust, and feel compelled to study the effects of intergenerational traumas. My own daughter conducted hours of videotaped interviews with my mother and pumped her for information about my parents' past. There was both an informal and a formal intergenerational transfer of memory between my mother and her granddaughter, and I have had ample evidence that the information was genuinely absorbed.

My daughter was not alone in such pursuit. In 2006, Aaron Biterman started a Facebook group for grandchildren of the Holocaust that had more than 2000 members in 2012.[2]

While the Holocaust unquestionably had an impact on how I have constructed the narrative of my being, given the abundance of information about the Holocaust easily available, I had qualms about contributing material about my personal experiences. When embarking on the writing of this book, I realized from the very start that for many the Holocaust meant suffering beyond imagination, and that I shall never know its psychological and physical costs, nor will I ever know all that my parents' eyes saw during the war, or fathom the fears, ordeals, and emotional traumas they experienced. I also did not rule out the possibility that my parents' experiences may not have been unique. Nonetheless, I had a very strong motivation to leave a record of my parents' lives and of my admiration for them as individuals who overcame the horrors of war and the subsequent repeated "transplantations" and displacements.

My parents' experiences, the stories they told me, and their written testimonies were not the only stimuli that compelled me to write this book. Other seemingly accidental sources contributed as well. Among them were some readings: Jan Karski's riveting account of his futile attempts to

---

[2] Suzanne Kurtz, "Survivors' Grandchildren Feeling an Obligation to Share Holocaust Memories," *The Buffalo Jewish Review* (April 27, 2012): 2.

alert Western governments to the horrors of what he had witnessed in the Warsaw Ghetto, for example, disturbed me deeply.[3] Reading the suicide note of Szmul Zygelboim, the Bund representative to the Polish National Council in Exile (in London), who killed himself in 1943 in protest of the world's indifference to the plight of the murdered Jews, had an even more powerful impact. His note read, in part:

> I cannot continue to live and to be silent while the remnants of Polish Jewry, whose representative I am, are being murdered. My comrades in the Warsaw Ghetto fell with arms in their hands in the last heroic battle. I was not permitted to fall like them, but I belong to them, to their mass grave. By my death I wish to give expression to my most profound protest against the inaction in which the world watches and permits the destruction of the Jewish people. I know that there is no great value to the life of a man, especially today. But since I did not succeed in achieving it in my lifetime, perhaps I shall be able by my death to contribute to the arousing from lethargy of those who could and must act in order so that even now, perhaps at the last moment, the handful of Polish Jews who are still alive can be saved from certain destruction....[4]

Zygelboim's words moved me profoundly, haunted me for years, and may be partially responsible for my writing this book. I wanted to leave some traces—however minimal—of my ancestors. My parents being the sole survivors of their families, I have never known my grandparents, aunts, uncles, or cousins. My losses include 70 relatives on my mother's side, and an unknown number on my father's side. The man I married was a war orphan, who did not discover a single relative after the war, and so I did not even acquire a family through marriage. I have felt a profound sense of the tragedy of my relatives' destruction and a moral obligation to ensure their survival at least in human memory and history, and that is why I have mentioned in this volume relatives I never had the opportunity to meet. Every echo of their existence contributed to my sense of honoring them, added a bit to my "pre-history," and helped me anchor myself in the past.

---

[3] Jan Karski, *Wielkie mocarstwa wobec Polski, 1919-1945: od Wersalu do Jalty* (Warsaw: PIW, 1992).

[4] Fern Allen, *Dramas of Jewish Living Throughout the Ages* (Jerusalem: Hebrew University of Jerusalem Press, 2005), 260.

The obligation to leave a record also struck me with particular force when I took a group of American students to Auschwitz in 1993. What shocked me when we first arrived at the death camp was the blatant commercialization of the site. At the time (it has changed since), when one entered, one walked first into a cafeteria and a souvenir shop. As my students proceeded on the guided tour, they saw clean, well-swept streets and tidy museum pavilions. The tourists in other groups often cracked jokes and chatted casually. I could see that my students were absorbing the sterility of the location, and that our guide was incapable of conveying the horror of what had taken place in Auschwitz. Until I prodded him, he did not even mention that Jews constituted more than 90% of the roughly 1.5 million victims exterminated in the camp. Despite my request, we were not taken to the Jewish pavilion: I was told that we ran out of time. My students got a sanitized history lesson and came away with hardly any sense of the persistent reality of death and the horrific mass murder in the extermination camp. After the visit, I supplied my students with additional information augmenting the guide's account, but I also realized the crucial importance of written records to counteract such superficial presentations. That obligation struck me as even more imperative in light of the recurring Holocaust denials, which are likely to continue, perhaps even intensify, given the dwindling number of eyewitnesses.

Am I hopeful that the lessons of the Holocaust are lasting, that they will be absorbed and will change the world? No, I am not. While we experience constant changes, both internal and external (technological, social, political, even climate changes), the fundamental human capacity to do evil has not changed. As the French proverb goes, "*Plus ça change, plus ça la même chose*" (The more things change, the more they remain the same).

The daily reports of ambushes, explosions, shootings, terrorist attacks, and wars all over the world make it harder and harder to ignore them and to wring a normal life out of the chaos. The enormity of concomitant human suffering presses on one's consciousness, and the world seems to be growing ever more chaotic and ominous. Perhaps one has to internalize Ralph Waldo Emerson's wise dictum: "He has not learned the lessons of life who does not every day surmount a fear."

* * *

The job of a literary critic, as I know all too well—having been one myself—is to analyze and judge. Yet sometimes critics ignore the legitimacy of the Rashomon effect: events and people may genuinely be perceived differently by various individuals. And the Roshomon effect applies also to the inner, private, personal perceptions of the children of Shoah survivors, to their responses as well as the responses of the readers of their texts. Not infrequently, children of Holocaust survivors are accused of being motivated by an egomaniacal impulse, of being narcissistic, of appropriating their parents' experiences, of being attention-starved and staking a claim on their readers or audiences for attention and sympathy. They are accused of writing their texts for self-serving purposes and with the intent of self-aggrandizement or self-promotion.

A few months ago, still in the midst of writing the manuscript for this book, I happened upon Ruth Franklin's collection of essays, *A Thousand Darknesses: Lies and Truth in Holocaust Fiction*, in which she strenuously drives this point home.[5] And Ruth Franklin is not alone.

Judging these second-generation writers is daring but not always fair. It is risky to generalize and even more risky to presume one can fathom another person's psyche or motives. As the Russian saying goes, "*чужая душа потёмки*" (Another person's soul is darkness).

I do recognize that total abandonment of the self may be impossible in any undertaking, but while there is some indulgence in any autobiographical writing, there may be selfless motivations as well.

Reading the testimonials of other children of Holocaust survivors—whether documentary or literary—I had the impression that for most of them the writing comes from a different impetus and different need than self-aggrandizement. They *have* been marked by their parents' wartime experiences, however these were conveyed to them.

---

[5] Ruth Franklin, *A Thousand Darknesses: Lies and Truth in Holocaust Fiction* (Oxford: Oxford University Press, 2011).
  I must admit that this book impressed me on many counts. While Ruth Franklin is a sharp and perceptive reader, and most of her essays on works written by survivors are excellent and probing, and I also fully share her dismissal and objections to fraudulent Holocaust memoirs, some of her judgments concerning the writings authored by children of Holocaust survivors struck me as excessively harsh.

Conclusion

The images that come to the minds of the "second generation," the metaphors and associations related to Shoah which they convey in their writings, most certainly stem from a very personal absorption of their legacy. In Teresa Torańska's book *Jesteśmy* (We Are Here), a collection of interviews with children of Holocaust survivors who left Poland following the events of 1968, I found a number of pertinent statements to that effect. Danuta Biterman expressed it poignantly and tersely:

My wszyscy—napewno każdy z nas ci to mówi—zostaliśmy wychowani z sześcioma millionami zamordowanych na barkach. Z wyrwą nie do zapełnienia. W jednych domach o tym się mówiło, w innych nie mówiło, ale to było bez znaczenia. I tak wiedzieliśmy.

(All of us—each of us certainly tells you this—we grew up with the murdered six million on our shoulders, with a gap impossible to fill. In some homes it was spoken about, in others it wasn't, but this was irrelevant. We knew anyway.)[6]

The Polish writer Agata Tuszyńska, who discovered at age 19 that her mother was Jewish, felt compelled some years later to research her family history, which resulted in the book *Rodzinna historia lęku* (A Family History of Fear, 2008). In a recent interview she reiterated that she still carries within her the "odziedziczony podświadomie po mamie starch" (fear subconsciously inherited from her mother) and the overall "*odziedziczony wojenny lęk*" (inherited wartime dread).[7]

This legacy often surfaces in visions and dreams. In another interview included in Toranska's book, Wanda Gruber stated the following:

Jako dziecko bałam się iść spać. Śniła mi się wojna i Niemcy wyskakiwali zza każdego krzaka. Chyba przez książki. Dom był zalany książkami, dużo wojennej literatury. Chyba czytałam. Nie pamiętam. Nie było u nas żadnych zakazów, co mogę czytać, a czego nie mogę.

---

[6] Teresa Torańska, *Jesteśmy: Rozstania 68* (Warsaw: Swiat książki, 2008), 376.

[7] Interview with Agata Tuszynska, Wysokie Obcasy, http://www.wysokieobcasy.pl/wysokieobcasy/1,100958,13039236,Agata_Tuszynska__nigdy_nie_zaczynam_pisac_od_pierwszego.html?as=4

(As a child I was afraid to go to sleep. I dreamed of the war and the Germans were jumping from behind every bush. It must have been because of the books. Our home was flooded with books, lots of wartime literature. I must have read it. I don't remember. There were no prohibitions in our house as to what I could read and what I could not.)[8]

Another vivid account of the "acquired" anxieties surfacing in dreams, and the powerful urge to leave a record, can be found in Marta Fuchs' autobiographical book *Legacy of Rescue: A Daughter's Tribute*.[9] The author's mother, Ilona, a Hungarian Jew, survived Auschwitz, while her father, Miksa Fuchs, survived forced labor. Here is one of the author's dreams. Her reflections concerning it follow:

I am preparing to go into the Holocaust with full knowledge of the horror that had happened during it. I am at once in the beginning of it and after it. I am rushing about trying to gather what would be the most useful and durable clothes to take for such an ordeal, which pants would be the strongest, which shoes would be the most comfortable and last as long as possible, trying quickly to put them on and take an extra set in order to join the others who have already left. And I must catch up with them or else I will be lost.

I wake up instantly. Details of my dream swirl and pound inside me, demanding immediate attention. Trembling, I know I have experienced something deep, sacred. I watch the images replay before me as messages burst forth with meaning. My need to catch up with everyone is my need and sense of urgency to get the stories from the survivors in my family while they are still alive. Once they are gone, I fear I might be lost without them. I belong with them and perhaps should die off with them, too. Henry [her brother] and I talk about not quite feeling second generation but rather in between, having one foot in each, the bridge between. Is it because we were born in the Old Country [Hungary], speak the language, spent our childhood in the land where it all happened?[10]

---

[8] Teresa Torańska, *Jesteśmy*, 270.

[9] Csaladnak Press, 2011.

[10] Marta Fuchs, *Legacy of Rescue: A Daughter's Tribute* (Albany, CA: Csaladnak Press, 2011), 104.

I can strongly relate to this account and have no basis to question its sincerity. I, too, have often felt "in between." This expressed itself in, among other things, my tendency to befriend older Holocaust survivors. To this day I am in touch with several very elderly persons with such a background. My inclination to keep in touch with them may seem puzzling because these interactions are largely depressing. It stems from a mixture of protectiveness and an impulse to offer some compensatory support, but also—I have to admit—from a sense of psychic comfort in their presence because I know that they know who I am and what my emotional burdens are.

Yet another passage from Marta Fuchs' book is worth adducing. It conveys a rumination she has as she walks with her children somewhere in California:

> I am walking across a supermarket's parking lot. It's prime time, just before dinnertime, and lots of cars are pulling in and out. I take Jacob's [her son's] hand and lift Sophie [her daughter] up in my arms for added safety. Suddenly, I see myself from the back and begin to have the image of all those women and children walking toward the gas chambers. A deep sadness overtakes me and my eyes well up with burning tears as an imploring wish comes over me: I hope that as they walked unknowingly to their deaths, the mothers were able to hold their children's hands and lift their children in their arms as I was doing now. I hope that the continuity of comfort would not be broken, that the mothers could continue being mothers to their children and the children could continue feeling enveloped by their mothers' love in those final moments of their lives.
>
> When I related this experience to a few friends and colleagues, they were gripped by the horror of it, yet it wasn't horror for me. It was a moment of grief mixed with gratefulness. A moment of mourning for all the mothers and children, my aunts and little cousins, my father's teenage niece whose name I bear. And a moment of gratitude, that here I am, a member of a generation that wasn't supposed to have been born, here with yet another generation I am able to, at least in this moment, protect and nurture.[11]

As this passage clearly reveals, the residual effects of the Holocaust need not be all negative. I, too, have had such mixed responses. Mindful

---

[11] Ibid., 100-101.

of the facts that my mother was repeatedly on the brink of starvation when carrying me in her womb, that she had to run to cellars and shelters when bombs were falling, that sustaining her Aryan cover took an enormous emotional toll, I have had for much of my life a profound sense of wonder and gratitude for being essentially both physically and mentally fit, for my body functioning properly despite my mother's stress and malnutrition during her wartime pregnancy.

More recently, when watching the film "Fateless" based on Imre Kertesz's autobiographical novel, I was deeply disturbed by a scene in which an emaciated young boy has an infected, swollen knee, is unable to walk, and while being transported in a wheelbarrow looks at the sky. What was he thinking then?, I wondered. Did he feel anger at God? The persistent question again crossed my mind: how could a civilized European nation inflict such suffering on children? Yet after I left the movie theater and I looked at the blue North Carolina sky, I also had an overwhelming feeling of gratitude for my avoidance of suffering and for the many blessings in my life.

Even some of my sudden associations frequently come from that pool of second-hand yet profoundly felt experiences, and are not all negative. For decades now, I have thought that my life has been a miracle. And so was my parents' survival. When I walk on cobblestones or red brick sidewalks and see a weed which despite all odds managed to break through a crack, I am often moved. For me that image of the delicate green leaves grasping for sun is symbolic. I think then of the many plants that were destroyed in the process of building the street or sidewalk, of the many seeds suppressed under the weight of the pavement, of how they were never expected to sprout. The image becomes a metaphor for my parents' vulnerability during the Holocaust and their staying alive against all odds.

My parents' survival and my coming into this world despite the vicissitudes of wartime were miraculous enough, but even the first years of my life played out against the background of Europe in upheaval. While the war ended when I was four months old, the westward shift of Polish borders, the massive moves and transplantations of populations from Poland's former eastern territories, and the influx of Jews who survived the war in the Soviet Union, then the Cold War and the ideological rifts between East and West, all of these created volatile conditions for several decades. My parents witnessed all of these events.

Conclusion

The author, Warsaw, Umschlagplatz, 2006

* * *

Writing this book was not easy: I was assailed by hesitations and apprehensions about sharing some very personal stories; about the degree of openness I could allow myself. I have finally written it encouraged by several friends, but also by a statement made by Rafael Scharf during an International Conference on the History and Culture of Polish Jewry held in Jerusalem. His words were: "Every footprint, each document, each scrap of paper, each trace in whatever form, is valuable beyond measure for a nation whose roots give sense to its history and whose memory of the past vouchsafes the continuity of its existence."[12]

* * *

This book is primarily a "Kaddish" for my parents. Yet I do hope that my account goes beyond their story, beyond my family's history, and sheds some light on the lingering legacy of the Holocaust.

---

12 Antony Polonsky, ed., *"My Brother's Keeper?": Recent Polish Debates on the Holocaust* (Oxford: Routledge, 1990),195.

LIFE GOES ON...

My daughter Hanna and her family, September 2012.

My son Ben and his wife Lise
on their wedding day,
October 4, 2012

INDEX

Afula 73
Albagli, Andre Nudel 110
Albagli, Henrique 110
Albagli, Michel Camel 110
Albagli, Rafael Camel 110
Albagli, Ruth 110
Albagli, Shlomo 110
Albright, Madeleine 115
Alexander, Eben 107
 Life Beyond Death 107
Amer, Mr. 44, 46-7, 51
Amer, Mrs. 47
America *see* United States
Amherst 124
Argentina 123-4, 130
Ariel, Rachel 8
Armia Krajowa 122
Association des Ecrivains de Langue Francaise 124
Athens 81
Auschwitz 16, 150, 154, 168, 171, 174
Austria 85
Aviron, Rifka (Pinczuk) 21, 34, 103-4, 108, 111, 130-2, 134-5
Aviron, Sura 130

Bat Galim 75
Beethoven 30
Begin, Menachem 131
Belarus 20, 67

Belgium 112, 159
Benjamin, Walter 14
Bereza Kartuska 11, 50, 113, 119
Bereziacy 113
Berger, Ronald J. 154
 Constructing a Collective Memory of the Holocaust 154
Berlin 83, 142
Bernstein, Leonard 150
 "Kaddish" Symphony No. 3 150
Bet Erdstein 75
Bettelheim, Bruno 149
Bialystok 31, 33-4, 38-40, 44-5, 48-9, 51-8, 62, 101, 103-4, 122, 140
Binghamton 90-1, 93-8
Bisłowska 38-40
Biterman, Aaron 169
Biterman, Danuta 173
Blavatsky 106
Bjaček, Petr 95
Boston Globe 114
Boulevard Brune 144
Brajterman, Shana Sura 110
Brazil 110
Broadway 98
Brooklyn 93-4, 98
Bryl, Andrzej 78
Brynów 69-70
Brześć 10, 20, 29-30, 39, 48-9, 52, 56, 62, 67, 100-5, 113, 117, 119-20, 130-2, 134, 140

Brześć ghetto   25, 49, 52, 103-4, 107, 120, 141
Buffalo   8, 63, 105, 112, 139
Buryevyestnik   134
Bytom   67-8, 119-20

California   90, 175
Canada   123-4
Carpathian Mountains   80
Casablanca   81
Celle-beim-Hanover   30
Centre National de Recherche Scientifique   11, 123
Chernovitz   74
Clifton, Lucille   16
  "The Past Was Waiting for Me"   16
Cohen, Arthur   152
Cold War   176
College for Foreign Languages   83, 87, 90
Communist Union of Polish Youth (KZMP)   118
"Concept of a Hero in Bernard Malamud's Writings, The"   90
Cwirko-Godycki, Anna   9
Czechoslovakia   115

Dachau   150
Danuta   144-7
Derbyshire, William   97
Dickinson, Emily   108
Dresden   83
Drugie pokolenie   169
Dubno   59, 61, 66-7, 106

Egypt   89
Einsatz   53
Einstein, Albert   106
Ellis Island   111
Emerson, Ralph Waldo   171
Engelking, Barbara   149
  Holocaust and Memory   149
Engels   71

England   82, 155
Epstein, Helen   153-4
  Children of the Holocaust   154
  Where She Came From   154
Europe   14, 73-4, 140, 148, 166, 176

Fammarion, Camille   106
  Premonitory Dreams and Divination of the Future   106
Filipcyk, Dr.   48
Folks Sztyme   78, 93
Frajlich, Anna   9, 155-6
  "Eva's Tree"   155
France   11, 81, 86, 91-2, 97, 111-12, 123-4, 137, 144-7, 158
Franklin, Ruth   172
  Thousand Darknesses, A   172
Fuchs, Marta   8, 174-5
  Legacy of Rescue   174
Fuchs, Miksa   174
Fulbright Scholar   89-90, 99

Gates, Henry Louis   159
Gdańsk   92
Gdynia   81
Genoa   34, 72
Germany   32, 34-5, 41, 53, 81, 83, 91, 93, 123, 155
Gershwin, George   71
  "Porgy and Bess"   71
Gestapo   20, 39-40, 49, 55, 120-1
Gimazium Finkla   118
Gliksztejn, Ida   119
Gliwice   68
Gomułka, Władysław   89
Graz   97
Great Britain   82
Grebler, Anat   74, 114
Greece   81
Grol, Halina   11, 68
Grol, Marek   117, 142
Grol, Regina   10-11
  "Anchored in Ether?"   11, 165

"Unde Bonum?" 164
"Walking on Pain" 166
"Walking the Streets of Warsaw" 162
"Why?" 163
Grol, Sarah 112
Grol, Tovyeh (Teofil) 10-11, 48, 61, 106, 111, 116-18, 121
   C'est arrive en Pologne 11, 122
   Geshtaltn un Perzenlehkaytn in der Yiddisher un Velt Geshihte 123
   "How Homer Saved My Life" 112
Gross, Jan 153
   Neighbors, The 153
Gruber, Wanda 84, 173
Gruda, Ilona 119
   Rachela 119
Grynberg, Henryk 84
Grzegżołko, Mrs. 21-3, 25

Haifa 72-3, 75, 78, 81, 91, 106, 168
Haifa University 168
Haley, Alex 159
   Roots 159
Heaney, Seamus 148
Hebrew Immigration Society 34, 95
Hirsch, Marianne 156
   Family Frames 156
Hitler 16, 36, 83
Hoffman, Eva 8, 151
   "Ceremony, The" 8, 153
Holocaust 12, 14-17, 63, 76, 88, 105, 114-15, 117, 125, 140, 148-57, 159-60, 168-9, 171, 174-7
Homer 106, 112
   Iliad 112
Hungary 74, 174

Israel 11, 14, 17, 34-5, 72-3, 75-81, 89-91, 93, 109, 112, 117, 125, 128, 130-1, 136-7, 168
Istanbul 81
Italy 11, 72, 81, 91, 95-6, 110, 116, 122, 139, 146, 158
Izmir 81

Janicka-Powell, Irena 155
Javits, Jacob 95
Jedwabne 8, 57, 153
Jerusalem 125
Jerusalem University 112
Jewish Historical Institute 119
Judenrat 119
July Manifesto (*Manifest lipcowy PKWN*) 66

Kacyzne, Alter 8, 129, 142-3
Kahn, Sy 90
Kamińska, Ida 83-4
Kamińska, Ruth 84
Karski, Jan 169
Katowice 11, 68-71, 119, 123, 135-6
Katz, Janina 150-1, 157
   Abram 157
Keff, Bozena 152-3
   Utwor o matce i ojczyźnie 152
Kennedy, John F. 98
Kerry, John 114
Kertesz, Imre 176
Khrushchev, Nikita 72
Kiel 81
Kielce 34
King, Martin Luther, Jr. 98
Kiriat Binyamin 73
Kiriat Eliezer 73-5
Koch, Ed 125
Kolki 128
Konar, Ala 98
Konar, Wlodek 98
Kotarbinski, Tadeusz 118
Kovel 62, 66, 102, 119-20, 134, 160
Kozlowsky, Mr. 30-2
Kraków 99, 152-3

Latowicz, Karol 84

Lejzor (uncle) 26
Lenin 71, 82
Leningrad 82, 101
le Pen, Jean-Marie 145
Lepzeig 83
Levi 128
Liberowa, Mrs. 79
Lopatis 111-13
Lopatis, Chaim 113
Lopates, Gela 111, 113
Luz, Claudia 110
Lvov 129, 136

Majdanek 150
Majeris 41-8, 53, 56
Malamud, Bernard 90
Marseille 91
Marx, Karl 71
Maryla 48-9
May, Karl 118
Meissen 83
Melman, Marian 83
Melman, Wiktor 83
Meyer, Hermann 18, 26-7, 29-36, 38, 40, 56, 140
Mickiewicz, Adam 128, 148
  Forefather's Eve, The 128, 148
Middle East 125
Milgrom, Felix 63
Morocco 81
Moscow 82, 131
Moshav Timmorim 125
Mount Carmel 72, 74-5
Muranów 78

Nalewajkówna, Maria 24-5, 30-1, 41-2
Naples 34
New York 38, 86, 91-5, 105, 112, 125-6, 139, 155
New York Times 107, 126
Nirenblat, Inda 25
Nirenblat, Leon 136

Nirenblat, Szlomo 136
Nixon 96
NPR 38
Nudel, Calkie 110
Nudel, Gela 108, 117-18, 120
Nudel, Mojzesz 117, 120
Nudel, Sura 118

ORMO 87
Oz-Salzberger, Fania 114

Pakistan 126
Palestine 117, 119, 122, 131
Paris 11, 91, 93, 95, 106, 123-4, 137-40, 144-7, 158
Pawlowska, Mrs. 79
Pearl, Daniel 126
Perugia 116
Pinczuk, Aluś 125
Pinczuk, Chaja 25, 100-3, 132, 134, 142, 159
Pinczuk, Israel 130
Pinczuk, Jankiel 135-6
Pinczuk, Lejb 20-1, 28, 108, 129-30, 135, 142-3
Pinczuk, Malkil 52, 101-3, 132, 142
Pinczuk, Masza 10-11, 20-35, 56, 61, 128
Pinczuk, Mojsze 28, 108, 128-9, 142-3
Pinczuk, Szalom 25, 101-2
Pinczuk, Szlomo 20-1, 130-2, 135, 142-3
Pinczuk, Szymon 135-6
Pinsker, Sanford 154
Piraeus 81
Pisar, Samuel 150
Plato 106
Poland 10-11, 17, 20, 34-5, 49, 66-7, 71-2, 74-81, 83-99, 110-12, 114, 116-7, 122-3, 126, 129, 135-7, 144, 149, 152, 169, 173, 176

Polin: Studies in Polish Jewry 8
Polish Committee of National
    Liberation 66
Polish National Digital Archive 119
Pomeraniec, Cypa 101, 142
Poronin 80
Potapow 51-2
Prague 92, 115
Presse Nouvelle 123
Protocols of the Elders of Zion, The 89

Rawicz, Maja 79
Rawicz, Wanda 79
Retig, Abraham Samuel 84
Rigg, Bryan Mark 36
    Hitler's Jewish Soldiers 36
Rio de Janeiro 110-11
Rita 74
Rome 84, 95, 166
Rouen 81, 86, 92
Rumania 74
Russia 123

Sady Zoliborskie 78
Salvin, Mr. 79
Sao Paulo 110
Sas, Dr. 69
Scharf, Rafael 177
Schellenberg, Dr. 45-8, 50, 53, 140
Schrider 26-7, 29, 31, 33-4
Shakespeare 107
Siberia 27, 101-3
Silesia 67-8, 71, 77, 136
Simoncini, Gabriele 118
Singer, I. B. 119
Six Day War 90, 125
Social and Cultural Jewish Society
    (TSKŻ) 78, 80
Sophocles 148
  Antigone 148
South Africa 124
Soviet Union 11, 57, 66, 72, 88, 92,
    134-5, 176

Spain 112
Spiegelman, Art 153
  Maus: A Survivor's Tale 153
SS Oliwa 81
SS *Rotterdam* 86, 92-3
St. Petersburg 101, 117, 129
Stalin 71-2
Starzyńska, Mrs. 79
Starzyński, Stefan 79
State University of New York (SUNY)
    90, 93, 96
Students for Democratic Society 96
Szochet, Hasia 136

Tamarkina, Rosa 131
Tashkent 136
Teachers' College 78, 88
Tel Aviv 125
Tenenblat, Szmul 93
Tenzer, Anna 93-4
Tenzer, Moniek 93-4
Thaler, M. Michael 150
Torańska, Teresa 84, 173
  Jesteśmy: Rozstania '68 84, 173
Towarzystwo Społeczno-Kulturalne
    Żydów w Polsce 11
Treblinka 119
Trudzia 70
Trybuna Ludu 89
Turkey 81
Tuszyńska, Agata 157, 173
  Łęczyca 157
  Rodzinna historia lęku 173

Ukraine 11, 66, 74, 77, 110, 128, 136
United Nations 168
United States 11, 14, 38, 82-7, 89-99,
    110, 114-15, 123-6, 138-40,
    146-7, 155, 167
University of Haifa 75
University of Perugia 95
University of the Pacific 90
University of Toronto 159

Vienna   17-18, 34-6, 72, 84-5, 95
Vilno   121
Volhynia   59

Wall Street Journal   126
Wardi, Dina   151
  Memorial Candles   151
Warsaw   10, 49-50, 52, 61-2, 66-7, 77-9, 82-3, 90-5, 99, 116-17, 119, 131, 136, 144, 162, 166, 170
Warsaw Ghetto Uprising   88, 170
Warsaw Polytechnic Institute   87
Warsaw University   10, 66, 79-80, 83-4, 87, 89, 96, 109, 118
Wąsowicz, Mrs.   53-5
Wawrzyniak, Mrs.   53
Węgorzyno   80
Wiesel, Elie   150, 154
  Jew Today, A   154
Wilde, Oscar   126
World War I   56
World War II   10, 14, 17, 34, 60, 77, 79, 85, 88, 97, 114, 119, 153
Wysokie Litewskie   23, 25-6, 28, 32, 35, 38-9, 49, 52, 56, 62, 119, 121, 128-9, 142

Yad Vashem   111, 142
Yiddish Book Center   124
Yiddish Theater   83-4
Yugoslavia   81

Zabinka   132
Zajac, Anna   85
Zajac, Wladyslaw   85
Zakopane   80
Zapasiewicz, Mrs.   79
Zapasiewicz, Zbigniew   79
Zeisel, Irit   74
Zolibórz   78
Zosia   74
Zygelboim, Szmul   170
Zylberblat, Pelta   101, 129
Zylberblat, Pola   33

www.ingramcontent.com/pod-product-compliance
Lightning Source LLC
Chambersburg PA
CBHW051128160426
43195CB00014B/2384